MW01245371

Coach, Caddy, Ref

(My 50 Years in Sports)

MIKE REED

Copyright © 2023 Mike Reed
All rights reserved
First Edition

Fulton Books
Meadville, PA

Published by Fulton Books 2023

ISBN 9 979-8-88731-294-1 (paperback)
ISBN 979-8-88731-295-8 (digital)

Printed in the United States of America

INTRODUCTION

I have been involved in playing and coaching baseball (Little League through Major League), golf (caddying from clubs to the PGA and LPGA Tour), and basketball officiating (youth leagues to the NBA and World Basketball League).

While I was going through chemotherapy, I had a lot of time and decided to put my stories into print. After posting several of my stories on social media, I was encouraged to put them all together into a book. This is the result. I have been involved in the MLB, NBA, WBL, LPGA, PGA, and high school and college playing and coaching baseball throughout my life. These are a small collection of my stories and memories over the past fifty years.

I have tried to keep this book on the humorous side. I also have tried to leave out the names of some of the people who these stories would embarrass. I have excluded most political stories except for ones that developed me as a person or were entertaining.

I would like to thank my brother Kerry and my many friends over the years that helped make this possible. I would also like to thank my three ex-wives: Jeannie, Cindy, and Margaret who have put up with me over the years. I am far from perfect and have made many mistakes, but being with these three allowed many of these stories to become true. The stories are told to the best of my memory. Anything vulgar has been left out.

I hope you enjoy reading them as much as I have living and then being able to write about them.

THE BEGINNING

I am going to start my book backward, to explain how it all came to be.

Several years ago, I was coaching baseball at Liberty High School in Hillsboro, Oregon. After a game was over, I was putting away equipment into a small storage shed. I must have bumped something because a rake came off the wall and hit me on my right temple. Other than feeling extremely stupid and dazed, I continued putting the equipment away.

A couple of weeks later, as I was moving to a new apartment, I walked down the ramp from the rented truck to my new garage. Although I had my head lowered to clear it, I walked into the top of the garage door and, once again, hit the same spot on my right temple. This time, I went down like I had caught a right-hand punch from Mike Tyson.

The next morning, my right eye was blurry. After a couple of weeks of bearing it, I decided to get it checked out by a doctor. He recommended me to a specialist. The specialist, Dr. Paul Tlucek, did several tests. In one of them, he held my eyelid down while flashing a high-powered light into my eye. This lasted for what seemed an eternity. I told him, jokingly, that I would have told him anything he asked and that that method should be used in all police interrogations. He told me that he found that my retina was torn as he was plotting the inside of my eye. I now had a choice to make. It was right before the start of high school basketball, and I was planning on officiating. He told me that the blows to the head usually do not cause a retina to tear, so I was perplexed as to how it really happened.

I talked to Dr. Paul and asked if I could work the year without doing any damage. He said I could.

I talked to the Portland Basketball Officials commissioner, Steve Scott, to let him know that I would only be working with one eye. He seemed unworried and said that it did not matter. I coached baseball that spring at Scappoose High School and finally decided, after the season, to have the operation. I returned to Dr. Paul to talk about it. When he told me that they normally have the person awake during the procedure, I told him emphatically: "No way! Knock me out and then do whatever you want." The surgery was scheduled.

When I checked in, I was still very apprehensive about having this done. My blood pressure was through the roof, as a result. They gave me something to lower it, and off I went to the operating room. When I was in the operating room, I told the nurse, "I have seen enough. It is time to go to sleep!"

When I woke up after surgery, I was informed that I could not go above 1,300 feet for a month. I learned that I had a gas bubble in my eye, and it would explode if I did not comply. I was not allowed to pick up anything over ten pounds, which meant my dog had to jump up to my bed on his own. I also had to lie facedown for a week. I was allowed to get up and go to the bathroom with my head down but, then, right back to bed. I learned that it was not a good experience watching TV with a mirror on the floor aimed at the TV.

Watching the gas bubble dissipate was like watching the needle on a car's gas gauge go slowly down. Finally, it was all over. At the time, we were moving from Hillsboro to San Diego, and it took a while for the new insurance to kick in.

Once insured after a month of being in San Diego, I went to see Dr. Murthry about the previous high blood pressure. I was losing weight rapidly and was peeing a little blood once in a while. I justified that it was because I had passed a couple of kidney stones. The doctor ran several tests, and she found something in my urine. She said to come back in two weeks and, then, get tested again to make sure it was just an infection. When I went back, it was still there. She recommended me to a urologist, Dr. McIntyre, who said I needed a CT scan. Not ever having one of these, I imagined that I would get a hypodermic the size of the Seattle Space Needle injected into me. Anxiously, I did not sleep all night. I went in the next morning nervous as heck. I found out that, instead of the huge needle that I had imagined, they put a small IV into my wrist to put the fluid through that. It was extremely simple and painless. I asked the tech if he found anything, and he told me that he was not allowed to say anything, according to protocol. As a result of the scan, Dr. McIntyre called me and scheduled a cystoscopy. It sounded fairly harmless, so the time was set. This was in April 2018.

I went in for the cystoscopy appointment and was told to put on a gown. I then was told to lie down on the table. I tried not to look around the room because I do not like to see, in advance, what Henry VIII torture devices would be used on me. Dr. McIntyre and his nurse came in. They rubbed some numbing agent on me. The doctor then said I might feel a little pain. Little did I know that my urethra was about to become the eastbound entrance to the Holland Tunnel. I almost came flying off the table when the NBC camera attached a rubber tube that was inserted into my urethra. It seemed like hours as it made its journey inside of me. They kept saying, "Breathe deep," but that did not help. When it reached the prostrate, it felt like I had been prodded with a log. Finally it reached my bladder. Dr. McIntyre asked if I would like to see it on the screen.

I said, "Hell no, get that thing out of me!"

The journey out was no better than the entry. He asked if I had played sports because I had a lot of scar tissue in my urethra. I said yes, I had been hit there several times. He finally came out and said, "You have cancer."

My mind started wandering. He was talking, but I do not remember much. He said that the tumor was the size of a golf ball and needed to come out. I asked if I could wait until the baseball season was over because I wanted to coach one last year.

I told the staff at Francis Parker (where I was coaching) and could not have been treated better. Several of the coaches in the league found out, and I actually had a couple of them pray for me on the field before our games; it was very moving. I have always been a Mets fan and wanted to see them one last time just in case the party was over. They were playing in Phoenix at the end of May. One of my fellow coaches at Parker, Erick Threets, had played for the Diamondbacks. He was able to get me a ticket to one of the games. After our last game at Parker in the middle of May, I told the kids. It was very emotional because I did not know if that would be the last I ever was on a field. I went to see the Mets, and the surgery was scheduled for early June.

When I arrived for check-in, they did all the paperwork, and my blood pressure was bouncing again, which was to be expected. They took me back and got me ready. This whole experience made me examine my entire life. It brought me back to my beliefs in God. I was praying while this was going on, not knowing if I would ever wake up again. I was finally put to sleep. I woke up in intensive care. Needless to say, my prayers had been answered, but I did not know the extent of the surgery. I started talking to the nurse, who was taking care of me, and I discovered that she was the wife of the assistant athletic director at Parker. It really is a small world. Dr. McIntyre then came in. Dr. Mac is an old-school Navy doctor, who has no time for nonsense. We talked about his golf game for a minute as he knew I had caddied professionally. He then told me that the tumor was bigger than he expected, he got it all scraped out, and he had administered my first dose of chemo. He said he was able to save my bladder, but it was close. My prayers had been answered. He then said that normally people go home at this point, but because of the amount of work he had to do and the way I was bleeding, I would be staying overnight. He also said that the chemo I needed was in high demand due to a shortage across the United States and would be a couple of weeks until it came in. He told me that he had cleaned out my urethra. I was wheeled upstairs a while later.

I was out of it for a few hours. I had a catheter in, and that was something new for me. About six o'clock, my nurse came in and asked if she could bring me something to eat. It was the best sandwich ever. At about 9:00 p.m., she came back in and asked if I needed anything else. I told her I was lying in bed, The Padres game was on TV. I did not have to get up to pee, and they were bringing me food; life could not get any better. She laughed and said I was the best patient ever.

At about 4:00 a.m., another nurse came in and said it was time to walk. Whatever self-pride I had was soon to go down the road. I got up wearing the gown with the back open, my butt hanging outside. I was holding on to the support with my catheter bag attached. I was wearing hospital slippers. I took my stroll back and forth down the halls, not really caring anymore because I was still alive. The next day I went home and was scheduled to have the catheter out in four days, the longest four days of my life.

I went in to have the catheter procedure done. The nurse said to breathe in and out, and the next thing I know, she pulled on it, and it was out. When it hit the prostrate, I once again jumped. It was finally out. It took about a month for the chemo to arrive.

I was scheduled for six treatments every Thursday for six weeks. I was coaching junior-high football at the time. The chemo treatments are done the same as the cystoscopy and the surgery, right up the urethra. It did not hurt anything like before. Afterward, I had to go home and lie down for two hours, turning every fifteen minutes to coat the inside of my bladder. Once the two hours had passed, it was like a hazmat cleaning in the bathroom to get rid of the chemo. After peeing, I had to dump bleach into the water and let it sit for fifteen minutes. This had to be done every time I peed, for four hours. I finally finished the treatments, not missing any games or practices. Since it was done through my bladder, I did not lose any hair, although I could have used that as an excuse for diminishing hairline.

I was scheduled for another cystoscopy. It had been a while since the chemo had ended, and the fear of cancer coming back was always there. It was the same as before, and now I knew what was coming. It felt like the camera had now been downgraded from studio size to home-use size. It hurt again as it passed the prostrate. It finally reached the bladder, and Dr. Mc said it looked like the cancer was all gone. He asked if I wanted to see, and this time, I said, "Why not?"

He told me that it looked really good and was still going to have me do three more chemos. I told him that it was a walk in the park.

I had to wait for the chemo because there was still a shortage. Two months later, COVID-19 arrived, and everything was canceled.

During the lockdown, I started to write down some old stories about playing, coaching, and officiating. I was sharing them on Facebook and got great responses. It was suggested that I write a book about them, and after some thinking, I decided to do it. I have not heard from my doctor for over two years. Whatever happens now is out of my hands. I have had no symptoms, and my weight has maintained at the level that I want.

These are stories from the fifty-five years that I have been involved in sports. I hope you find them entertaining. Back to the beginning...

CHAPTER 1

1955 to 1969

I was born in Lebanon, Oregon, on August 7, 1955, to Wallace and Louise Reed. My mother had been adopted (more on that later in the book) by Al and Linnea Love, who both were Swedish immigrants and met in the United States. My dad's parents were Milo and Bertha Reed, who also lived in Lebanon.

I attended Santiam Elementary School (grades 1–6) in Lebanon. We had a softball-throwing contest that I won in second or third grade. Back in the sixties, the World Series was always played during the day. I used to sneak a transistor radio into the classroom and listen to the games with an earpiece. It was very tricky sometimes, getting away with it. And looking back, I would guess most of my teachers knew what I was doing. In 1965, the Yankees were playing the Cardinals. I wanted to stay home and watch the game, but my mother said no. I begrudgingly went to school. About an hour before it was supposed to start, I told the teacher that I was not feeling well. I was sent to the office, where they called my mother. She came and picked me up. When we got home, she checked my temperature. It was normal. She asked me why I told them I was sick. I said I told them I wasn't feeling well because I wanted to watch the game. I was allowed to put the pajamas back on and watch the game. A year later, my teacher was doing a lesson for class, and I was not paying attention. She walked over to see what I was doing and saw that I was keeping score of a game being played at recess. I have always been addicted to baseball.

The sixties were tough. I remember the day JFK was assassinated. The principal came on the intercom crying and announced that the president had been shot and that we were all to go home immediately. I lived about a mile from school, and it was one of the longest walks of my life. Everyone was very upset. I saw Oswald get shot on live TV. It was very hard to deal with. I had great teachers that discussed the events without interjecting their own personal beliefs.

I grew up in a great neighborhood. Ronnie Benshoof lived next door to me. He had a rock band in high school, and they practiced every day. There were nights when I turned off the music just to listen to them play, and I think the other guys in his band still play. Mike Grenz's grandmother lived across the street from us, and he was there quite a lot. Ralph Sherman lived next door to them and Lonnie Straney next door to Ralph. We all played together and got along great. If we were not playing soldiers, we were playing baseball somewhere. I remember one day at Mike's house he had a relative there who must have been five or six and was being obnoxious. Mike picked up a football and threw a Tom Brady-like spiral that hit the kid directly between the eyes. The kid went down crying but did not act up again. It was hilarious.

I spent the early summer days from fifth grade through tenth getting up at 5:00 a.m. and picking berries and then beans with my grandfather so that we could have money for my brother, sister, and myself for school clothes. The family was on government assistance, so we got the dreaded gubment cheese, peanut butter, and day-old bread. You could not melt the cheese with a blowtorch. The peanut butter had enough oil in the top of the can to lube your engine, and the day-old bread could have made an excellent Frisbee. It wasn't much, but we got by and it did not hurt one bit. My parents did the best they could.

When I was in sixth grade, we had a substitute teacher. A couple of us decided to change our names. The teacher took roll, and none of us answered. She finally asked me what my name was. I made up the name Arnie Watson and told her I was a new student. Later in the day, something happened, and she called the office over the intercom, saying she was sending Arnie Watson to the office. The office said, who? I went to the office, and they called my mother. It was the last time I *ever* went to any school office.

I always listened to AM radio. I learned the title and artist of each and every song. The local radio station was KGAL in Lebanon. They used to have contests giving away records, movie tickets, and other items. I won so many contests that they put in a rule about only being able to win so many times in a month. One day as I was listening, the DJ announced that I had won a contest. I called because I had not entered anything. The DJ had misplaced one of his lists, and he knew that I had it written down. He gave me a free-bie for helping him out. Sixties music was a wonderful time to live through. I remember watching the Beatles for the first time on Ed Sullivan. My dad (who loved old country and Western) hated it. He always called them the "Longhairs." The first record I ever purchase was "Between the Buttons" from the Rolling Stones.

I attended Lebanon Junior High across the street from Santiam in grades seven and eight. I played basketball but was small and horrible defensively. Baseball was my calling. I started on the eighth-grade team as a seventh grader. My dad had mentioned to another player's dad that I wanted to play in the MLB. That got back to the kids, and my new nickname was Pro. I did not like it, but it could have been worse. During the summer, I played and made a couple of all-star teams. We did not have fancy uniforms, just a T-shirt and jeans. Because my dad was disabled very early, we had no extra money for anything extra. The local sporting-goods store Bill & Cap's allowed me to buy a glove on a layaway program where I would pay them a little every week.

Back in those days during PE, we all had to dress down in uni-form, and after, everyone had to shower. We were banned from snap-ping towels. On this particular day, Eddie Beam, who was a rather large boy, was busted snapping a towel. The teacher had a "hack" paddle to deal with these instances. The paddle looked like it had come from a Viking ship and its previous job was an oar. Eddie was told to bend over and grab his ankles. I remember hearing the impact and watching his butt move for a minute with the aftershock. It was at that time I decided that I would never incur the wrath of any PE teacher.

My mother used to work occasionally at Sharon's Restaurant. Every once in a while, she would bring home extra food. On this particular night, it was Salisbury steak. My brother despised that entrée. As most of the families back then did, we all ate together. My brother refused to eat it. This was approximately at 5:00 p.m. At 8:00 p.m. he was still seated, looking at the cold food. We had no microwave then, and it was now a power of wills. My mom kept telling him he would eat it, or he would sit there. Nine p.m. came, and it was bedtime. My mom finally sent him to bed. He had won the battle. It was the last time Salisbury steak ever reared its ugly head.

In eighth grade, we were playing dodgeball in PE. I broke the pinky on my nonthrowing left hand. That did not stop me from playing baseball. I had a heavy splint on it but kept playing. Earlier that year, I was riding my bike and not looking to see what was in front of me. I did my best Evel Knievel impression, going over a VW Bug and crashing. I should have had stitches in my leg, but that would have kept me out of playing for a couple of weeks. I just put a Band-Aid over it and kept going, and I still have the scar.

Back when I was growing up, my mom and dad used to drive me and my brother to Portland to watch Blazers games. They would visit relatives and pick us up after in a designated spot at a designated time; we did not need cell phones. One night, the Blazers were playing the Golden State Warriors. Back then, we used to get autographs on the game programs. The players stayed across the street from the coliseum. After the game, we went down to the player entrance and waited. Warriors center Nate Thurmond came out and we asked him to sign.

He said, "It's too cold to take my hands out of my pocket."

It was in December, and it was cold. My brother and I looked at each other and took off running. We were in the lobby of the hotel when Nate walked in. We asked again for his autograph as he was one of our favorites.

He said, "You two are persistent little shits."

He then signed for both of us. It was a classic.

CHAPTER 2

The High School Years: 1969 to 1973

I decided to play basketball in the winter of my freshman team. We had two teams that were divided equally. I was chosen to play on the Chiefs (our mascot were the Warriors). My coach was Lytle Cowell. Coach Cowell was from Arkansas, and he stood about five feet and six inches and weighed 225 pounds. He scared the hell out of all of us.

Coach Cowell had developed his own offense called the "Cowell Cyclone." The offense was set up against man-to-man defenses and was comprised of screens and fast passes. We had a parents' night when everyone attended, and each team played a scrimmage. I screwed up the offense, and the whistle blew. Coach Cowell gave me complete butt thrashing. I was hoping a crater would open, and I would fall into it. I stood there and took it. It was the last time I ever messed it up. The more I played for the man, the more I realized how much he actually loved all of us, and it was his way of making us better players. I would have run through a wall for this man.

Later in my senior year, I was the scorekeeper/manager for the team. The team was going to Hawaii for Christmas and he invited me to come along. I could not believe it. We left Christmas Day for Oahu, where we would stay with players and play two to three games. We arrived that afternoon. I remember spending Christmas Day watching Deliverance at a downtown movie theater. I also ran into Rodney Dangerfield coming out of the hotel.

The next day, we met the players. I was selected to stay at the home of Mackey Feary. We hit it off right away, and his family treated

5

me like I had known them for years. Mackey was into drugs at that time. I have never used any, but that did not stop us from being friends. We left after a few days, and I lost contact with Mackey. He went on to be the lead singer for the group Kalapana. He later committed suicide after a long struggle with drugs. I was saddened to hear it and still remember the good in him. RIP, my friend.

Lebanon hired a new head baseball coach during my freshman year. Bill Croco was brought in to coach the team. I played freshman baseball with his son Bill. We became friends along with another baseball player, Kevin Brannon. Brannon decided that we needed to play Strat-O-Matic Baseball. We played it all the time. We had a schedule that we played and kept statistics. One night, we had a marathon at my house that went on for twenty-four hours. I learned how to manage from that game. We had our own language that developed from it. Back then, we all wore black shoes and had a can of black shoe polish in the dressing room for our shoes. The freshmen were always careful to stay clear of any seniors because they liked to paint their butts black. When we showered, it was always fast. I got it one time and figured it was a rite of passage. You cannot do that anymore.

The summer of my freshman year, I was selected to play on the junior state team, which was a very big deal. The coach was Dick Weisbrodt. Coach Weisbrodt was one of the all-time high school wrestling coaches in Oregon and was also an outstanding baseball umpire. One night, we were playing Corvallis, one of our main rivals. I struck out to end the game with the tying and winning runs on base. I was livid after. My mom had enough and took me to Coach's house. Coach told me that I did not cost them the game. Games have so much that happens over the course of a season that there are many instances that affect the outcome; one play may have been big, but it was not the only reason. I learned a lot from him. He was also my math teacher my sophomore year and coached me again in the summer of my sophomore and junior years. I was a younger player, and since I had been hurt (story coming up), I stayed back a year to rehab.

We usually had the same bus driver for all of our away sports. Our bus driver, Jay D, was one of a kind. On one particular trip, we were making a lot of noise on the way home. Jay turned the blinkers on and pulled off I-5. He stood up on the bus and made the statement "if you guys do not shut up, I am going to drive the bus off the road and kill every one of us." An immediate silence took over the bus. We all believed him and never again did anyone make any noise, win or lose.

In the summer of my sophomore year, I was hired by the city to maintain the youth fields. I would go with another guy who could drive, and we would take care of the fields all day. It was a great job where I developed my love for working on them. I stopped playing basketball my sophomore year and played in church league. My grandfather used to take me to those games, and he always watched every baseball game I played, never saying a word after no matter how I played.

During my sophomore year, I met Terry Henderson, who was a freshman. Terry was named Bullhead. Terry had a massive cranium. His mom used to cut out the back of his baseball hat and put it in elastic so that it would fit. Terry is also the only player I have ever seen wear fishing lures on his game hat. And now for some Bullhead stories.

Bullhead and I used to go fishing. One morning, we were headed up to fish the Santiam River above Sweet Home. At about 5:00 a.m., he turned on his blinker, and we pulled off into the parking lot of a very small fishing store. A sign on the door said, "Knock on the door, we are always open." About ten minutes passed, and Bullhead emerged from the store. He got into the car, and I asked him what he bought. He said a bobber for $0.5. We were fishing in a river; bobbers were not used. He did it to wake them up.

On the opening day of my senior year, we were scheduled to play on a Saturday. Bullhead was a no-show as he told Coach Croco he was sick. On Monday, the *Albany Democrat Herald* had a picture on the front page. The caption was "Terry Henderson of Lebanon pictured fishing at Freeway Lakes on opening day." It did not go over well. After this, he became Bullhead the Magnificent. This is the last and most memorable story. We were playing a night game in Legion Baseball. Terry had a shutout in the top of the seventh inning. Some guy in the opposing dugout made a comment about his head size. He proceeded to walk the next three batters on twelve pitches, nothing closer than the top of the head.

Coach Croco came out and had me come in from the right field to finish the game. The guy that had popped off to him was the next batter. Bullhead told me as he left the mound that if I did not hit him, he would get me after he got him. I got the last three outs without allowing a run. After the last out, that kid had gone sprinting to the parking lot. The only thing that saved him was that Bullhead was in the right field and not the fleetest of foot to catch him. He laughed after. We used to stop and eat after games. We went to the Dairy Queen in Stayton (it is still there), and Terry ordered a Brazier Burger, 57 triple D with nipples as big as pancakes. We all lost it, and the poor girl could not stop laughing.

I was playing basketball in PE in my junior year. I went up to catch a pass, came down, and my knee went the wrong way. I knew immediately that it was bad. My mom took me to see our family doctor. He decided to drain my knee. It was one of the most painful things I had ever done. It took three syringes full to get out the fluid. He left the needle in each time, and it would bounce off the bone. That was the only time in my life that my mom was not offended by swearing. I would rather have three teeth pulled with needle nose pliers than that again.

My parents then scheduled me to see an orthopedic surgeon. I had to have dye shot into my knee. I had torn my ACL and lateral meniscus, and I messed up my kneecap. I was scheduled for surgery. In those days, they made you check in the night before. The next morning the nurse came in and said it was time. She gave me the shot. It felt like she had walked across the street, climbed to the tenth floor, and fired a hunting rifle at me. I came straight out of the bed. They wheeled me into surgery, and I was still awake. I saw what looked like the shelf at Home Depot of power tools and told the nurse that I had enough, please put me to sleep.

I was supposed to have a recovery time of five to six months. It was the start of baseball season. My goal was to lift sixty pounds fifteen times with that knee before I could play. I hit the room every day, and after two months I was cleared to play. That was why I stayed back at junior state that summer.

My senior year was entertaining. A group of us created a Guts Up League. This was always two on two. We started with football. We played no matter what the conditions. We also would sneak into Parker Stadium, where the Oregon State Beavers played every Thanksgiving, Christmas, and New Year's Day. We jumped the back fence, and off we went. Guts Up continued into basketball season. We had about six teams and played in all weather conditions. When I was not doing this, I was playing baseball. We played a massive amount of Wiffle ball.

The backyard of my house was pretty big. I used to mow it to make it look like a baseball field. It had an incline in the middle and was like the old Reds field, Crossley Field. I wanted to install lights, but my dad would not let us. Instead, we would go to the tennis courts and play around the nets. They had lights, so we always had to bring quarters. We also played two-base double or nothing at my old grade school, Santiam. The wall of the gym was used as the left and part of the center field. It was about forty feet high, and we called it the Beige Monster, after Fenway Park. The right field was out of play. We would take BP before the games and always used baseball bats that we had broken during games. I can only imagine how many hundreds of balls they found when they went up there.

We used wood bats up to my senior year. We used to go to Salem to a sporting-goods store. The basement of the store was all wood bats. We could pick out any MLB player's bat and weigh it. I had several different styles for any type of pitcher that we would face. I would take a Coke bottle to the handle, then apply massive amounts of pine tar. Once before a game, Brannon, Croco, and I walked into our locker room where we had all the bats prepped and ready to go. The bats were gone, and we were pissed. They were finally tracked down in the office of Bud Moynihan, our athletic director. He told Coach Croco he took them because we defaced school property. He told them we had bought them. After that, our athletic director was called Baseball Bat Bud, and we made sure our bats were hidden.

Our senior awards were held at the Elks Lodge. We had the banquet room right next to the bar. There was a partition separating them. Once our awards started, a drunken lady at the bar started laughing. It went on for the duration of the awards. Over the course of the baseball season, we kept the names of any ugly guy we played. We had read Jim Bouton's book *Ball Four* and got the idea of an All Ugly Nine. The MUP (most ugly player) was the third baseman from Sweet Home we referred to as Baby Toklat. He was horrid.

I struggled with the bat my senior year but wanted to play in college. I went on a visit to Lewis & Clark College in Portland and decided that was the place for me and that I would at least get the opportunity to play. Because my parents were in a bad financial state, I received a lot of financial aid and work study.

CHAPTER 3

The College Years: 1974 to 1977

I entered Lewis & Clark in Portland, Oregon, as a just-turned eighteen-year-old. I was quite ill-informed about everything in the world as I had grown up in a pretty protective environment. The day I was dropped off at college was tough as I had not been away from my parents for any period of time. I met my roommate, Rick Hennessy. Rick was a local from Cleveland High School and played football and baseball. We hit it off right away. I was on a work-study scholarship, and the baseball coach (Mickey Hergert) at school was also on the football staff. He asked me to be one of the trainers/managers for the football team. I said yes.

I started the first week of school. Fred Wilson was the head football coach. I would compare Fred to Woody Hayes, the great Ohio State coach. Fred usually smoked a cigar and had a lot of one-liners. Bill Seamon was the head trainer and had a business in equipment repair. Everything went pretty well, but I had a lot to learn. The practice was down in a valley, and it was a lot of stairs to go up and down. I made many trips because something was usually left above, and I was the one to get it. I got to go on road trips with the team. The first year, I rode with Bill as we took all the equipment in his van.

Over the course of four years, a lot happened. We were in a restaurant in Central Washington, and the waitress came on the intercom asking for Mike Hunt from the Lewis & Clark football team to please come to the counter as it was an emergency call. Every time she announced it, we would crack up laughing. Finally, two of the players came in and said they were the callers.

Our bus broke down on the interstate between Pendleton and Portland, and we had players at two in the morning hitchhiking back home. During my last year there, Fred had a zero-alcohol policy. That included those over twenty-one. We had taken the train to Bellingham, Washington. The team lost the game, and the next morning several were passed out on the bags waiting for the train. Fred was livid. A team meeting was called on Monday. Fred asked everyone who had a drink in the last week or so to raise their hand. After the count, sixteen (if I remember correctly) were left. He dismissed the rest of the team.

We had to play our rivals Linfield the next week. They were loaded. Because we did not have enough players to run two teams in practice, I quarterbacked the scout team. I was asked by Ray Baker to play, but because I had not played before and had knee surgery, I did not think that would be a smart idea.

Just a quick story about Ray. He used to coach the linemen. He would take them into the squash court, blindfold them while wearing helmets, and put boxing gloves on them. It was a Roman-gladiator event and was hilarious. You could never do that now.

Back to the Linfield game. We had several players playing both ways, my roommate Rick included. They beat us up badly, but our guys did not quit. If memory serves correct, we played one more game, and then the season was called because we lost a couple more to injuries.

In the winter, I was the trainer/manager for the basketball team. The head coach was Dean Sempert, and he was a funny guy. I usually roomed with him on road trips, and he always made me laugh with a dry sense of humor. I only did that for one year.

The spring finally came along. Our team was split between seniors and freshmen and not a lot in between. We were short of pitchers, so Mickey decided to make me a pitcher because I threw so hard. It was learning on the fly as neither he nor his assistant, Greg Lord, were pitching guys.

Coach Lord was one of the funniest, most passionate baseball guys I have ever met. He had a temper that would immediately pop up, and we all loved him for it. He used to throw his hat down and then quickly kick it when it hit the ground. The bullpen pitchers would do the same thing after he did it, which was hilarious. Coach Lord would usually drive the van the veterans rode in. After the first year, I would ride with him. We were allotted meal money and usually played pinochle for it on the trips. There was one trip to Spokane, and a guy drove up next to us, and his car was covered in carpet. Coach Lord landed on the horn, and we are all in hysterics. Another time, Coach was driving, and we were cut off by a lady. I was riding shotgun, and he told me to throw an orange at her that was sitting on the dashboard. Being young and stupid, I obliged. I got her on the shoulder at a traffic light. She had no idea where it came from. Looking back now, not a good thing to do.

I did not make the spring-training trip to California, so I stayed behind trying to get better at pitching. When the team returned, we played the University of Portland at UP. They were a D1 team. They were hitting us pretty good, and I was told to warm up. I was brought in the third inning to pitch with the bases loaded. UP had two all-Americans, Bill Mebisius and Craig Deardorff. Guess who I got to face? I struck Mebisius out and was thinking that the pitching stuff was pretty easy.

Deardorff shattered that illusion when he hit a bomb off the left center field fence for a bases-clearing double. My first college at bat was against George Fox. I singled into the hole and beat it out on a rainy night. My first start was against Portland State, another D1 team. I hit a ball at Sckavone Park (very short fences) that was gone. Their center fielder reached up over the fence and took it away from me.

I had a very hard time learning to throw certain pitches over the course of a couple of years. My control was sporadic. In the summer, I pitched lights out; I just struggled during the school year. In the Fall League, I had a five-inning perfect game and was removed for another pitcher. I threw a two-hitter in a nine-inning game against the Portland State JV. Those were as close to no-no's as I would come. In my junior year, we played the University of Oregon. We hit two home runs in a row off their number one. The next batter for us, Jim Traut, took a fastball under the eye. It was a bloody mess. Their pitcher was acting like an ass and not concerned. I was pitching at the time and immediately hit the first batter. I got a couple of outs and hit another, but it was unintentional. The Ducks were yapping.

On another occasion we were in Lewiston, Idaho, playing national powerhouse Lewis-Clark State College. They were beating us badly, and I was brought in. I got two outs and threw a curveball to one of their players. I hit him in the head. He staggered to first. He got a lead, and I threw over. I hit him this time on the butt. He stole second. I tried to pick him off and, once again, hit him in the leg. He stood up and said, "Man, what did I ever do to you?" I still laugh to this day.

My only college save came against Portland State at Civic Stadium. I was brought into a game where we led 3–0 in the eighth with one out and a man on first. I got a double play on the first batter and retired the side in order in the ninth. That was probably my best moment in four years at L & C. On a side note, we played a lot at the stadium. They had a giant Jantzen lady on the wall in LF. The pitchers used to hit flies to the OFs after infield. I learned to fungo there and my specialty was trying to hit the lady in the breasts. I became quite good at it.

Dorm life was interesting. I lived on campus all 4 years. I had great roommates. We loved pulling pranks on people and back then it was not as stuffy as it is now. At L & C, the library is walking distance away from the lower campus dorms. It is a dimly lit, cobblestone road. One of the football players, Kevin Baird, had a red devil's mask. One of our favorites was to have a couple of guys rustle the bushes, and then one of us would jump out wearing a black cape and a mask. It was like watching a horror movie with screams. We did it to men and women. Our dorms were either male or female floors. We go to the ladies' floor, hide out in the phone booth, and one of us would go to another floor and call them. When the girl would go to answer, we would jump out. The screams were hilarious.

In my junior year, I lived in the dorms on the upper campus. We would usually yell "Snow!" late at night and watch the girls' dorm people look outside. They would see no snow, and we were mooning them. One night it did actually snow, and they were yelling, "No snow!"

Because of our actions that year, most of us were not allowed to live together the next year. It was like a real-life version of *Animal House*; we were out of control. There was a tunnel we discovered under all the dorms. Most knew nothing about it. We were able to go from dorm to dorm unnoticed. The area was tight, and I always felt like were in the movie *The Great Escape*. It was during dorm time that a fellow named Charlie LaPray transferred in. Charlie was a football player who had transferred from Oregon State. Rumor had it that he was so drunk one night that he fell out of a second-story dorm into a bunch of bushes and slept there all night. We devised a drinking scale that had various stages. The LaPray stage was one drink after you were already dead.

Drinking was prevalent during my college years. My roommate Dan Wright attended a party one Saturday night. The road he took home had two ninety-degree turns. He navigated the first but not the second. He went straight into a guy's yard, hitting a tree. The tree stopped him from going into the guy's house. Dan walked the rest of the way home, abandoning his car. He went back the next morning, and the police were there. They asked him what happened, and Dan's explanation was that he went to a late movie and was coming home when a small dog ran out in front of him, causing him to swerve.

The cop said, "That is BS, and you know it, but the smartest thing you did was walk away." Dan then proceeded to pick up all the black velvet caps in his back seat.

Back in my college days, we used to finish all our spring classes by noon as we traveled for baseball. Once the season was over, a lot of us would golf in the afternoon and then visit Multnomah Kennel Club (dog racing) at night. One night, I knew a dog was going to win the race. They had a trifecta wheel that cost $212, if I remember correctly. If we picked the dog to win, we had every other combination covered on a $2 bet. My roommate David Lowe was also the treasurer of our dorm. Since none of us had that much money, he "borrowed" it from the funds. The dog I picked won the race. One of the favorites finished second, and there was a photo finish for three. One of the dogs involved was the race's long shot. The other was another favorite. The long shot lost. We won about $400 and the dorm was repaid the next day. Who knows how much we would have made if the long shot came in. One other night, we decided to buy tickets to sit in the covered area. After a race, a guy sitting next to us had a heart attack and was carried out. The people at his table told us he had hit the trifecta for $7,000. We never found out if he passed away.

My senior year at Lewis & Clark College was 1977. The Blazers had won their first-round games and were now playing the Lakers in the West Finals. They announced that many tickets for games 3 and 4 would go on sale at 9:00 a.m. My two roommates and I decided to camp out overnight to get them. We were allowed four each for each game. The Blazers ended up winning games 1 and 2 in Los Angeles. Blazer fever was in full swing. We showed up the night before and were about twenty-fifth in line. Fortunately, it was not that cold overnight. I bought one great seat for myself and three in the upper section to sell. Back then, not all of the games were on TV, and although scalping was enforced, they were lax on it. I sold my extra three tickets for a *lot* of money through someone who knew I had them. The Blazers won both games and swept the Kareem-led Lakers. They went on to the finals against the 76ers, but I was not going to spend another night sleeping on the concrete at the Memorial Coliseum.

In my senior year, I student-taught at Jackson High School. My supervising teacher was Vic Carlson. Vic was an ex-football player. I was invited to play in the morning basketball game before school. There were several times I left there bloodied. The games were the WWE on steroids. It made me much tougher to play the game. That semester, I got a 4.0 for my grades. I ended up with a 3.2 GPA for four years, which was actually higher than my high school GPA of 3.16.

I had an interview to be the head baseball coach at Jewell High School. Jewell was a tiny community tucked into the mountains on the way to the Oregon Coast. This was my first interview. I walked in, and the entire school board was there, along with the principal and vice principal. It was pretty intimidating for a twenty-one-year-old. I did not get the job, so I moved back to Lebanon.

CHAPTER 4

The Lebanon Years: 1978 to 1979

After graduating, I moved back home. I wanted to learn to coach football, so I volunteered at the middle school. Don Grove was the head coach, and I learned a lot. There was a seventh-grader there named Bo Yates. Bo was the son of the high school head coach Gary Yates. Bo was a man among boys. There were teams who would not let some kids play against him. Bo went on to a fantastic high school career and ended up playing four years for Washington and head coach Don James.

I substituted for two years while looking for a head base-ball-coaching job. I taught every kind of class. Most of the time it was just babysitting but paid well, and I was in demand. I worked in the Lebanon and Albany school systems and could work every day that I wanted.

I helped coach the high school varsity team in the spring. We were playing in Salem one game, and the state penitentiary is located there. They had some low-risk prisoners that would umpire in the Salem association when they were short of officials. On this particu-lar occasion, we had one behind the plate. The calls were not good. Finally, I had enough. I made the comment "I don't know what you are in for, but you are killing us." Even he had to laugh at that one. I was then named the head coach for the junior state team in the summer. Those kids had played mainly on the JV team the prior spring. It was a great group of kids and parents. We hosted the state tournament at our field. I was the one responsible for all the fields, as well as taking care of the high school baseball field. There were many nights I had to get up at 3:00 a.m. to go to school to change the water. We had the long interlocking metal pipes that had to be manually changed. We won our first game but lost the next two. I learned a lot that summer.

The next summer, I had the junior state team again with a new group. These were 100 percent baseball kids. We had an eighteen-game winning streak and were playing a team in Eugene. It was the bottom of the seventh, and we were tied. The first batter reached first and eventually got to third with two outs. Having watched too much TV, I intentionally walked their number-seven and number-eight batters to reach the number nine. We walked him. The kid ran one-half to first, then ran off the field. I yelled at my kids to stay on the field. We did, got the ball, and appealed first. The batter was out, no run was scored, and we played another inning. We won it in the next inning. We eventually won twenty-six in a row before we lost. I still talk to kids who played on that team. Randy Gates, Jon Anderson, Brian McVein, and Phil Gilbert have all gone on to have very successful lives. I only hope I played a small part in them.

I then applied for and got the head baseball job at Woodburn.

CHAPTER 5

The Woodburn Years: 1979 to 1982

In the summer of 1979, I was the assistant American Legion baseball coach and head junior state coach. The Legion head coach was Bill Croco. He told me in July about a job opening in Woodburn. The athletic director at Woodburn was Dale Yuranek, Bill's best friend. I immediately called and got an interview. I had an interview with Dale and the principal, Peter McCallum. I thought it went very well, but I had others I also thought that went well, and I did not get the job. A couple of days passed, and Dale called me informing me that I had the head baseball job, teaching health and PE, and would be an assistant football coach. I was all fired up as Woodburn had won the state title a couple of years earlier with Tom Gorman pitching. Gorman eventually played with the Mets on the 1986 championship team. My mother was so excited that she called the local paper, and they published it before the Woodburn paper did.

I now had to find my first place to live by myself. I found a nice place a couple of miles from school. I moved in the first part of August, and two weeks later football started. From the start, the staff and the kids were outstandingly nice to me. I was very happy. School began. I was always told to be tough at first as I could always let up after, but it would not work the other way around. I gave the students my rules. I had a lot of students who asked to be transferred out to the other teachers' classes. After the first couple of months, the kids found out that I was not as bad as they thought. I had a lot who wanted back in. Back then, we did not have coed PE. It was either girls or boys in a class. I had one class of all girls, and it was interesting to say the least. The girls did not like dressing down, so they would use the excuse that it was their time of the month. I got wise to that very early. When they told me that, I had a red pen and would make a little red dot on that day. When they came back two weeks later trying to use that excuse again, I told them they needed to see their doctor because their cycle was messed up. That excuse stopped pretty quickly.

I coached freshman football with another PE teacher, Bill Rayon. He had the defense; I had the offense. We got along well, and Coach Yuranek gave us a lot of room to do what we wanted as long as we stayed in the framework. The varsity ran a power-eye formation. The kids we had on the frosh team were very talented. We ran a bunch of different offenses, including the wishbone and the run-and-shoot. If anyone was scouting us to use against the varsity, they would have gone nuts. We lost one game that year, 7–6 against Cascade. I loved the way the team played hard, and there were no bad attitudes among any of them. When the spring came, I found out that the team had lost a lot of seniors. We were young. It was a learning experiment for all of us. I had two pitchers who threw strikes, Lennie Wolfe and George Giles. I started a sophomore at first base, Scott Sowa, who was not blessed with any foot speed. My second baseman was Earle Ramsey. Earle threw batting practice for us as he only threw strikes.

We were hovering around the .500 mark and had a massive game against Gladstone. Our main field was grass, but on this day, it was not playable. We decided to play at the junior-high field. There was no fence. I decided to try something against them. I threw Ramsey against them. They kept hitting massive fly balls, and we were standing so deep that we caught everything. It was a tight, well-played game. In the top of the seventh in a tied game, they had the bases loaded with a full count on the batter. The batter swung at the pitch; it was low, and my catcher, Terry Withers, came up with it. The umpire called the batter out, and my team started running off the field. The batter was told to run to first. The runner on third scored. The umpires then got together and decided that the ball hit the dirt, and the runner was safe. I went nuts. I tried to protest the game but was informed that in Oregon High School games, protests were not allowed. We eventually lost that game.

The next day the home plate umpire did call me and told me he made a mistake and was sorry for it. You can never hold a grudge as he was human and man enough to admit it. We ended up having a decent year, and I was proud of my players.

In the summer, I coached the Legion team, the junior state team; pitched on the semipro team in Canby; and played slow-pitch softball. I was busy every night. I got ejected a few times over the summer as I have always had a problem with guys who do not know the rules. The Legion team ended up struggling to have players, so I had to play so the other eight kids could play. We called them exhibition games as I was obviously too old to play Legion. We played the McNary summer team at Chemeketa Community College. I came up early in the game with the bases loaded and hit one off the center field wall for a triple. It was 395 feet. That was the farthest I had a ball in competition. I was playing third baseman, and the opposing coach said to me, "How bad are we when the other coach is hitting bombs off us?"

In year two at Woodburn, I was moved up to JV football. I had the same kids as the year before, plus a few kids who played both JV and varsity. Like the year before, this was a great group. I was learning a lot from Coach Yuranek. This man was not old school; he was there before the old school was built. He was like a father to me. I spent many hours in his office learning how things were done. On one particular night, we were playing Gladstone. Our team was ahead 35–0 with about a minute to go. Gladstone had the ball on their ten with a fourth and ten to go, and they were going to go for it. Because they had been talking nonsense and hitting late, I called a time-out.

I could hear Yuranek in the press box, and he was pissed. We got the ball back and scored another TD, making the final 42–0. As soon as we left the field, Dale was waiting for me by the locker room door. Everyone went inside except me. Dale started yelling that it was the "bushest" thing he had ever seen and did not care why I did it. He went on for about five minutes and then finished. I said to myself that I would never do that again to any team, no matter what. The next night, the varsity played Gladstone. They ran the score up on us. It was worse than what we had done the night before. After the game, Dale asked me to step outside. He told me he was sorry that he yelled at me the night before and that the game had changed, and he hadn't. I had even more respect for the man after that, but it would not be the last time that he yelled at me.

Back when I started teaching, I substituted for Gary Yates at Lebanon High School a lot. We used to play dodgeball upstairs behind the bleachers, and it was an enclosed area with no place to hide. It truly is the best sports game ever invented as it combines every aspect of athletics as well as social interaction. When I went to Woodburn High School, I took it up a notch. We used PE classes that were boys or girls only. I taught both. In the boys' classes, I had to explain to Dale Yuranek and Principal Peter McCollum why I was having a two-week class. They both approved it. The classes caught on fast. I took white volleyballs and partially deflated them for maximum velocity. We could dodgeball when the balls were coming from one way, or prison ball where they were coming from front and back. Cheating and head shots were punished by the offender, doing five push-ups in the center, and they were season for both teams. I never had anyone not dressed down. It was the best exercise that any class could get. The classes became so popular that I would have boys from other classes come in and kids skip their lunches to play.

When I ended my career substitute teaching in the Hillsboro School District, I was allowed at some schools to play it, but we played with very soft balls. Those were coed classes, and most of the time, the girls were much better players than the boys. A lot of schools have now banned the game, which is a shame. I am guessing the same people who banned it were the ones hiding in the back, afraid to play.

In the spring, we were much improved. We had a big game against Cascade High School. They had always seen my little lefty Sean Sowa, who could not break a pane of glass but had a great curve and slider. I decided to play a trick on them. I would not give them my lineup until the coaches' meeting. I had my right-hander, Terry Shelton, warm up in the gym (I heard that the SF Giants did this and thought I would try it). It worked, we won, and when Yuranek found out about it, I was summoned to his office again. He went off on me, and it was deserved. I always loved the man because he did not hold back.

I had a young manager named Jeff Mathena, who was a great kid. I have always been superstitious. I do not step on any lines and always believed a game was never over. On one road trip, we were way ahead in the bottom of the eighth. I looked over, and Jeff had the bats all bagged up and ready to leave (back then we put everything into a bat bag). I immediately told him that if we gave up one run, he would be running home. He took all of them out and put them back. After the game, I explained to him why. He was a smart kid and understood.

My sister was getting married on a Saturday. We had a rescheduled game the same day. Back then, the coach always rode with the team. In this case, my JV coach rode the bus, and I drove down. The game went quickly, and when it ended I had to make the forty-five-minute drive to the wedding. I showed up right before it started, wearing my uniform in the back of the church. I missed many anniversaries and birthday parties over the years because I never wanted to miss any game. I took a lot of well-deserved heat for it, and if I could go back, I would have attended those events. There was always going to be another game but not those events.

In the summer, I played and pitched and coached the junior state team, which was going to be my varsity the next year. We had a very good summer, and things were looking great for the next spring. I played slow pitch every weekend as well as during the week. I played on several teams and sometimes on two different ones during the weekend. Being single, it was easy.

My last year at Woodburn was 1982. In the spring, we were having a live batting practice, and I was pitching. I threw a lot because if the kids could hit me, they could hit anything we played against. I never knew how hard I threw until I coached at Lewis & Clark. They had a gun one day, and I was clocked at ninety-three. Back to the scrimmage, I threw a fastball to one of my players, Brad Mendenhall. He ripped a line drive back at me. It hit me on the side of the head and was caught by the RF. I was out cold on the mound. I remember waking up in an ambulance. They took me to a doctor, and he said I was fine. I had to walk back to school (about a half mile) and was not feeling really good. I called my mom and told her what had happened. I lay down on the couch, and the next thing I knew my parents had driven and had the landlord open the door. They said they called many times, and I never answered. I went to the ER in Salem about thirty minutes away and had X-rays.

I ended up going to the Sowa's house, and they took great care of me. I was not able to teach the next day, but we had a game. Dale Yuranek said he would coach, but I never miss games or practices. I told the kids to make it fast because my head was killing me. They played great, and we got out of there very fast. Two weeks later, I was playing slow pitch and had a head-on collision with our left fielder. I wish we had concussion protocols back then.

It was after the first injury that I decided that I did not want to teach anymore and wanted to become a professional basketball referee. I submitted my resignation. I knew I would miss the kids and staff, but it was something I felt I needed to do. I was about ten hours away from my master's degree and never finished it. Looking back, I wish I had.

I am still in contact with a lot of the students that I coached and taught who are now adults. Jody Maxwell, Leo Ramos, Earle Ramsey, Gordon Postma, Jackie Karsseboom, George Giles, Jay and Jill Livingston, Jeff Grigorieff, Scott Sowa, Chris Cummings, Lennie Wolfe, and many more. Lennie went on to become a baseball coach, and there is a story later about that. I am very proud of the people that they have become. It was a different time, but I was very lucky to meet all of them.

After I left Woodburn, I was asked by Lewis & Clark baseball head coach Jerry Gatto to be his assistant. I was there for two years. I learned about life in general from the coach as he had a master's degree in psychology and used it every day. He was the most positive person I have ever met in my life. Jerry was famous for being thrifty. There were times in a game when we were short on balls, and he would reach into the warm-up ball bag and throw one out. These balls do not go as far as new ones.

We were having a scrimmage one day, and I was pitching. Bryon Henderson was the batter. I had grown up with Bryon as his uncle was Terry Henderson (Bullhead). Bryon was a left-handed hitter with exceptional power. I threw a hanging curveball right down the middle, and Bryon hit a ball that is still circling the Earth. He made sure to give me a bad time about it. He came up a couple of innings later, and I put the first pitch inside and knocked him off the plate. He was laughing, and the other players enjoyed it. Not many had seen a coach brush back a player, but I always had a competitive nature and just needed to send a message.

We were playing at Oregon State one day, and they were destroying us. After the fifth inning, Coach Gatto told me to make all the pitching changes as he was friends with the OSU coach and did not want to be seen again.

After I left Lewis & Clark, I got a job at a finance company in Vancouver, Washington. I moved up the chain and became an assistant manager. My job required a lot of collection work. I became very good at skip tracing. I found one woman in a hotel room in Edmonton, Canada; she could not believe it, but she did pay. There were many times I had to go to peoples' homes. Our office had one customer who had skipped and had his car as collateral. They could not find it. I told him I could get it back. I made a couple of calls, and it was repossessed the next day. The regional manager said it was unbelievable and wanted to know how I did it. I told him I had my "sources."

I also had to go to small claims court several times when we were forced to sue the borrower. I only lost one case and still cannot believe it. The woman had bought a vacuum with ninety days' free interest. After the ninety days, they had to pay it off or put it into a loan. The rate was 27 percent, and it was about $1,000. The judge said the finance rate was too high, even though the state of Washington allowed higher than that. He would not look at the laws and said she could return the vacuum. I really despised losing.

Our branch was required to have delinquency at 2 percent or less at the end of every month. One month, I had it down to .06 with only a couple of late accounts in the entire office. The regional manager called and said that it was too low; it was maybe the first time that ever happened.

One day I took a call from a headhunter who asked who did the collections at our business. I told him that I did, and he told me that a bank was looking for a collections officer. I interviewed and got the job. One of my main jobs was cleaning up some delinquent time-shares. I flew to Chicago for a meeting that had been arranged by a bunch of companies to get the time-shares back. I met a lot of great people and heard horror stories about the purchases. I eventually got all of them back, and they were sold to another bank. While I was at the bank, I was in charge of repossessions and foreclosures. I never liked foreclosing on anyone's home and was always happy to work with the people. I learned a valuable lesson that weekend—never buy a time-share.

The bank foreclosed on a beautiful home, and I had to go inspect it. The house had been used to make crack and meth. It had a horrible smell inside and locks on a lot of the doors. I did not know how they would ever get that smell out. On another occasion, the bank had a loan out with a local businessman. He kept promising to make payments but never did. He had a VW Bug as collateral. I had my repo man pick it up. The guy freaked out and paid the payoff. He then accused me of giving him a heart attack. It became apparent after a while that this was not the job that I wanted to make a career out of. I was let go for the first time in my life.

I needed a job, so I went back to the finance company that I had originally left. It was about this time that the World Basketball League started, and I was working early so that I could leave at noon for my five-hour drive to Vancouver, British Columbia. I would leave Vancouver at about 11 p.m. after the game. I used to line up three Pepsis and would have them down by the time I reached the US border. They would keep me awake. I would get home by 4:00 a.m. and sleep for three hours before going to work. That did not last very long as I wanted to be a professional referee and not wear a tie to work every day.

The finance company used to do sales contracts like the vacuum cleaner one I described above. We were required to do so many every month, and our business was down, so there was a lot of pressure to get business. A company called a loan application. I ran a credit bureau and could see that it was turned down by two of our competitors. The guy only had credit for six months, was twenty-one, and had opened three new credit cards. He did not qualify because of income-to-debt ratio. I turned it down per company guidelines. The branch manager looked at it and said I could combine all his accounts plus this one and approve it. I told him if I did that, the regional manager would fire me, and he said he would fire me if I would not. I said I was not doing it, and he fired me on the spot. I stopped by the regional manager's office after that, and he said they would move me to another branch. I told him I was not interested in finance anymore and went back to substitute teaching and officiating.

CHAPTER 6

The Playing Years

I started playing slow-pitch softball while at Woodburn High School. I was also still playing semipro baseball. It was quite demanding, but because I was not married, I played every day. I was playing 125 softball games a summer and another ten to fifteen baseball games where I would pitch. The stress on my arm finally reached a peak. We were playing in a tournament and lost our first game on Saturday. In double-elimination tournaments, that meant a very long way back through the losers bracket. On Sunday, after playing six straight games, I caught a ball in left field near the warning track and threw it home. It felt like my arm followed the ball on the way. I could not grip anything. That night I did not sleep and went to see a doctor. I was told that I tore my rotator cuff. The doctor said at my age there was no need to repair it because I was not going to play Major League Baseball. I ended up playing first base for the rest of that year. Ever since that happened, it has bothered me in cold weather, and I did not throw much.

My brother heard about a trick that put the game balls we used into a microwave for forty-five seconds. That method dried out the core of the ball, and they flew further. No one ever knew that he did it. For every game we played, each team provided the game balls. We always tried to use two of ours. Before every game, I would read a limerick (some were quite racy) from an old book my brother had found. It started out as just our team. When other teams saw and heard what we were doing, some of them started joining in. It eventually morphed into both teams, the umpires and even some of the fans joining in. It was hysterical. There was a young girl from Seattle…

One summer, my best friend Bob McCann was getting married. The ceremony was happening at his house in Albany with a reception after. I had a slow-pitch playoff game that night in Salem, so I did not drink anything. My brother made up for what I did not drink. He had nothing to do that night, so he rode along with me to the game. Once we were there, our coach and pitcher Raul Ramirez said that we did not have enough players and asked if my brother Kerry could play. I said sure, but he was pretty drunk at the time. We found an extra shirt and some shoes for him and put him in the right field. Raul said his name was Al, to take the place of one of the guys who was not there. The first ball that was hit to Kerry, I was yelling, "Kerry! Kerry! I mean, Al! Al!" at him from center field. He caught everything that came to him. He also had two hits in the game, and it was one of the best games he had played. He told this story to Donny Reynolds, who was a friend of ours, and Donny had one of the greatest lines of all time: "You can cure alcoholism, but you cannot cure great hitting." The legend of Al was born.

There used to be tournaments every weekend. They were all based on the teams' playing status. We started getting guys from all over our league who wanted to play for us. My brother had an "Al's" T-shirt made up that we always gave to anyone who played with us. Al's was written, and under it on the tail was "ringers." *Ringers* was a term used for guys brought in who were excellent players. The team ended up being an all-star team, and it was as fun as I ever had playing sports. We never had a problem filling our roster. To this day, I still call my brother Al.

Playing every day and all weekend, I played for a lot of teams and met a lot of people. One of the more colorful folks was a guy in Salem named Larry. He was a huge man. We ended up calling him Larry the Draft Horse. I played with Raul in many police-officer tournaments. He always said that my bat was deputized. I will never forget playing in Seattle and having a ball take a bad bounce in warm-ups, hitting me directly in the crotch. We did not wear cups, and I don't think this would have mattered. It was a valuable lesson I always told my players about. I could not play that entire day.

During my caddie years, I had gotten much stronger from carrying the bag. I came back to play church-league softball. I was always a gap hitter before, and now I was hitting 320-foot home runs. It was pretty amazing. I still could not throw much. I could really understand why upper-body strength was so important. I had fast hands and lived off that; I wish I would have done the extra work earlier in life.

When I returned to Oregon, I decided to play adult-league, over-forty baseball. My shoulder problems had diminished, and I was throwing a lot of batting practice to my players at LaSalle High School. I went to the tryouts as a fifty-four-year-old guy. I threw pretty well and was selected early. I was put on the Cardinals team. The Cardinals were a great group of guys. We did not win many games, but they were a fun group to play with. We were having a practice game before the season on a cold night. I threw, and once again, the shoulder popped. My pitching career was over. I had a great season playing first and ended up hitting over .500. I hit our only home run of the year. We rarely saw any velocity; it was usually just waiting until I could see something straight over the middle.

My last year of playing was a disaster physically. My arm was still hurting. During one game, I dove for a ball and broke my nose, and blood was everywhere. I continued to play. In a later game, I pulled both hamstrings. I finally decided I had abused my body enough and retired. I would throw batting practice to my teams once in a while but only when the temperature was warm.

I started coaching fast-pitch softball when my daughters started playing. My oldest, Megan, was very good. She tried out for a travel team in Virginia and made the team. It was a rough year. It was hard for me to be an observing parent. They never won a game on a Sunday in a tournament. The next year, all the coaches retired, and I took over the team. The team was made up of girls who had been cut from most of the other teams in the area. We started slowly but then won a few games. We were playing in a tournament and won our first game on Sunday morning. That had never happened with this group before. Our next game was against one of the best teams in Virginia, Fire & Ice. Our pitcher threw a one-to-zero shutout, walking no one and striking out no one. The only run was scored on my daughter's double. I had parents on the field crying, players were hugging everyone, and it looked like we had just won the World Series. I had never seen anything like it. Our next game was against the East Coast giants, the Shamrocks. The game was close and we lost, but that will always remain as one of the best games I have ever been associated with.

I was ejected several times over the course of coaching softball. Umpires who did not know the rules were always going to have a problem with me. We were playing in a showcase tournament at Virginia Beach. At the end of the morning game, the umpire told both coaches that it would be the last inning. We ended up tied. It was cold and drizzling. After the last out, he said we were going to play another inning. My pitcher had thrown seven innings and was tired. I did not have time to warm anyone up. The other team beat us, and I was livid. We played the next game immediately after and had the same umpire. He said there was a time limit, and I said no there wasn't. It ended up with me getting ejected at the captain's meeting.

On another occasion, we were playing in a tournament in Pennsylvania. The other team had a runner on first, and the batter hit a short fly behind my shortstop and third baseman. The ball came down and hit my shortstop's glove and went out of play. The umps correctly called dead ball. After that, they awarded the batter third base. I went out and asked why. The ump said because the batter had reached first. I told him that was impossible and irrelevant because it was a batted ball and you only get two bases. Once again he said she had first.

I said, "Okay, a batter hits the ball to left field, it hits the glove and then the ground and bounces over the fence, the runner already was at first."

The umpire said ground rule double. I told him it was the same thing; he once again said she was at first. After that, the hat got slammed down, and I was ejected again because of the umpire's incompetence. I told him on the way out that he awarded the first-ever ground rule triple.

We were playing in another tournament and were trailing by two runs in the bottom of the seventh. We had the bases loaded. My batter hit a line shot down the third baseline. The third baseman for the other team tried to catch it, but it deflected off her glove, and the sound could be heard—still went by third base in fair territory and then down the line. We scored three runs and thought we had won the game. The home plate umpire called foul ball. I asked him why. He said the ball hooked out foul, even though it still went by third fair. I asked the base umpire to help because he was closer. He said he did not hear anything. I then told them that "Blind and deaf are not good combinations for umpires." I was ejected again.

My team had qualified to play in the ASA Nationals at Johnson City, Tennessee. I drove six hours down and was tired when I arrived. It was about eight o'clock when I arrived. I decided to take a shower before bed and closed the shades on the windows before I went in, as I did not want someone seeing me naked and having a heart attack as a result. I went in, and when I came back, the curtains were open. Being tired, I thought I must have forgotten to close them. I went to sleep as we had an early practice the next day.

After practice, I returned to my room. I once again closed the curtains and went to shower. When I came out, they were open again. This time I knew that I closed them. I closed them again and went back to brush my teeth. I came out, and they were open again. I looked at the curtains to see if there was a spring in them to automatically open them. There wasn't. I closed them again and was peeking over my shoulder when the curtains flew open. I immediately knew to get out of there. I opened the room door, and as I did a cold, icy feeling went right through me. I was now freaked out. I went down to the front desk. I was obviously frazzled as one of the coaches saw me and said my hair was sticking up, and I was pale. I asked the front desk if they ever had reports of ghosts. He said they had as some people had been killed in a fire at the hotel many years ago. I asked to change rooms immediately as there was no way I was staying in that one. They moved me down the hall.

I grabbed a gurney and proceeded back to my room. My assistant coach and his wife heard the story and said they would help me get my stuff out. When I entered the room, the curtains were now closed (if you remember, they were open when I left). As they were throwing my items on the cart, the curtains came flying open. Carol (my assistant coach's wife) screamed and went running out. Donnie (my assistant) grabbed what was left and got out. The players on my team wanted to go in; I told them they could, but I was not going to again. I moved down the hall and had no more disturbances. I did not really believe in ghosts or spirits until this incident. It really opened my eyes.

After my divorce was final, I returned home to Portland and wanted to coach baseball again. I was hired at LaSalle High School to coach the freshmen. I was there for four years, becoming the head coach in my third year. One summer, we were playing Philomath in a summer league tournament in Newport, Oregon. They did not have enough players (it was a high school tournament), so they played some graduates against us. I did not care; we only wanted to play.

Their right fielder was six foot three and about 225 pounds, with a full-length beard. My high school kids were all baby-faced. My number-eight hitter was hitting less than .100 (he had one hit all summer). My number-nine hitter had a perfect .000 average. In the top of the second inning, the number-eight hitter got a hit; I should have run to the Lincoln City Casino and bet heavily after that.

The next batter, who was left-handed, got a pitch low and inside and proceeded to hit a home run to right field. My team went crazy, and so did his parents. He came up again at the bottom of the third. No one at this time. They threw him the same pitch, and he hit it again almost to the same spot, except this time the right fielder was deeper and caught the ball over the fence. He came again in the fifth, again following a double from my number-eight hitter. Same pitch again, and this time it went twenty feet over the fence. It was insane. The ten-run rule was in effect, and the game was called 5 innings. We were the last game that afternoon, and they had a home-run derby after. I asked Bradley if he was going to participate, and he told me no, he was saving them for the next day. This kid had *never* hit one before, and I had a better shot of becoming the Queen of England than he did of hitting another. I decided it was time to get him.

We played the first game the next day. I told the rest of my team to watch and say nothing. I talked to Newport's coach who was a friend of mine, and he was in on it. Bradley finally showed up still riding a high from the prior day. I was about to ruin his day. I said we needed to talk. We walked over by the concession stand but close enough so that my team could hear what was going on.

I said, "Bradley, you had the best game of your life yesterday."

He said, "Thanks, Coach, I am so happy."

I said, "Well, you know baseball is a business."

He said, "I know."

I told him that Newport's coach was very impressed, and they needed a quality left-handed hitter the following year. His eyes got bigger. I said that I traded him to Newport for a junior left-handed pitcher and a JV second baseman. His mouth was wide open, and he said, "I cannot believe that you did that."

I said again that it was a business. My team was cracking up and starting to fall over; they were laughing so hard. Bradley kept shaking his head in disbelief. I told him that I had to wait until the morning to announce it as the OSAA (Oregon's governing sports body) had to approve the trade. I said the Newport coach was up in the press box and wanted to talk to him.

Bradley walked upstairs, and it looked like the Bataan death march—he was moving so slowly. He was up there for a few minutes, when the Newport coach yelled down, "Coach, we have a problem. I walked up, and Bradley kept shaking his head."

Newport's coach said that he tried to tell him they won the state two times in the past four years and have a fantastic facility. Bradley said that his mom just had a new job and could not move. I said that they did not have to, Newport would help him with housing, and I did not trade his two brothers (both were in my program), only him. By now he was almost in tears, and Newport's coach had to turn away; he was laughing so hard. Finally I had to tell him.

I said, "Bradley, you do know that I cannot trade high school players, right?"

A smile came to his face.

I said, "You have got to be the most gullible human on the face of the planet."

I told his parents the story, and they loved it. This was one of many times I had done things to players and usually got the same result. Bradley helped me so many times his senior year setting up the press box and doing things for me. He was and is a great young man.

My second year as head coach ended in a very dramatic fashion. We made the state playoffs and had the first-round game at home. I saw Kurt Peterson in the stands before the game and briefly chatted with him. He was the father of one of my pitchers. We won the game, and I was at home when the phone rang late and my athletic director, Brian Crawford was on the line. That was never a good sign. He told me that Kurt had taken his life after our game. A lot of things ran through my head. The next day I found out that he had PTSD and was having bad episodes of it. The entire team attended his mass at school the day before our next game. Suddenly, baseball was not that important anymore. It really put everything into perspective, especially since I had lost my friend Peter Vicars years earlier. We played the next day and lost 5–4. It was a very tough game to coach and for the kids to play.

I had made a promise to myself that I would not get ejected during the high school season. It was hard sometimes to accomplish as we saw some very bad umpiring and calls. The school also received fines for any ejection, so I did not want that to come out of my paycheck. If you were ejected, you also had to sit out the next game. The summer was different—no fines and no suspension. We were playing and were on defense. There were no outs, and the bases were loaded. The batter hit a high pop-up, and it came directly down on the pitcher's mound. It was an obvious infield fly, but there was no call. The other team scored a run, and we got no out recorded. I went out and asked why. The umpire said it was a difficult catch, but that it had nothing to do with the call. I said just that because my pitcher could not catch, the batter was still out. Kurt Peterson's son Theo was the pitcher, and I could hear Kurt laughing. The final result was me being ejected for another umpire not knowing the rule.

It seems like I was always ejected during tournament games. We were hosting a tournament at LaSalle. We made it to the championship game, and I had specifically asked for good umpires for the game, no matter who was playing. Two guys, who I had never seen before, showed up. We were leading in the top of the sixth inning, and the other team had the bases loaded with two outs and a two-two count. The pitch was low, and their batter took a three-fourth swing and then pulled the bat up. No call from the home plate umpire. I asked for help; the first-base umpire was not even looking and said, "No swing."

The next pitch got hit to the fence, and they scored three runs. In the bottom of the inning, the others team's third baseman said to me that it was a horrible call and that their batter had swung. At that moment, the first-base umpire, who was across the field, came running across and said I could not discuss his call. I asked him how it was that he could hear us talking all the way across the field but could not see an obvious swing from being much closer. Once again, I was tossed. I was thrown out of a championship game on my field, and I had to actually pay these guys to the umpire. That was the last time I was ever ejected.

We moved to Hillsboro, and I decided to go back to substitute teaching. It took me a couple of months to get my license back, so I was a teacher's aide during this time. Once my license came, I was able to teach any subject at any level. I called substituting combat pay. A lot of junior-high and high school kids have their cell phones on during class. Most of the time, subbing is just giving them paperwork to do. In middle and elementary schools, you actually get to teach. I ended up doing first grade and kindergarten, as it was much more enjoyable. I could act like a kid, and they loved it. After I did it for a while, I would have requests from teachers I had worked for. Some days were much easier than others; it just depended on how much nonsense the kids were going to try. They found out very early that the things that they got away with other subs were not going to happen on my watch. It made for some long days, and I do not miss it one bit. I applaud the classroom teachers and substitutes for their hard work.

I went to Hillsboro High School after I left LaSalle. My pitching coach was former SF Giant Rob Dressler. Rob and I became great friends. The kids did not know who he was until one of them looked him online. Rob had a great sense of humor and always made me laugh. We were playing one of the teams in our league, St. Helens. Their pitcher had a different-colored sleeve on that was illegal, and I asked Rob to tell the umpire on the way by to have him remove it. The St. Helens fans went nuts and started yelling at Rob. He said a few things back. When he returned to the dugout, he told me that his career had hit rock bottom after being in a verbal altercation with them. I laughed for two innings after.

I had an outstanding center fielder named Roberto Virrueta. Roberto was extremely talented but also very stubborn sometimes. We were in the middle of a close game, and I tried to get him to move more toward left field three pitches in a row. Finally, I called time and took him out. I did not have many players on the bench, and I chose a young man named Dylan to take his place. Dylan looked like Dennis Eckersley. I call him Eck to Dressler. Baseball is not a forgiving sport. You cannot hide anyone on a baseball field. It is almost guaranteed that when you put someone in, the ball would be hit to them. The other team had two runners on. The batter hit an absolute rope to left center fiend. Dylan took off after it. I put my hat over my eyes and told Rob, "Tell me when it is over." I heard yelling and looked out to see Dylan make a one-hand running catch on the warning track. It still is in the top-three plays that I have had any players make, especially under the circumstances.

We played a game on a Saturday and came back Monday to play an away game. One of my players showed up wearing a turtleneck. It was a warm day, and I thought nothing about it. When we were getting on the bus, I noticed he had a rope burn underneath. When we arrived at the site, the bus driver told me that she had seen it and asked what I was going to do about it. We had no district guidelines to go by. She was upset with me. While the kids were warming up, I took the player aside and asked what happened. He told me that he had broken up with his girlfriend Saturday night and tried to hang himself. We talked for a while, and he told me that he really needed to be with us. I agreed. I put him in late in the game and he got a hit. When he was at first base, the other team's player asked him what happened, and he said that it was a long story.

The player's mom called me the next day and thanked me for what I had done. It meant the world to them. I knew that this was why I was in coaching and was proud of how the young man responded. A year later, I was substitute teaching at an alternative school, and he was there. He came up and gave me a hug and once again thanked me. I am glad I was in the right place at the right time.

After our freshman season had ended, the varsity team made the playoffs. At the time, Hillsboro was still in Oregon's largest classification. We were the twenty-ninth team rated out of thirty-two. All games would be on the road against the best in the state. The varsity had struggled all spring but once they got hot, they got hot. They took out three of the top five teams in the state. Head coach Matt Baillie did one of the finest coaching jobs I have seen in my career. He kept everything positive, and the team thrived off it. It really showed how much believing in yourself and your team can really get you. The season ended in a semifinal loss at Sheldon, where future Los Angeles Charger quarterback Justin Herbert played as a sophomore. He came and pitched the last inning and was very impressive. I would have loved to have seen how good he could have been at baseball, but he made the correct decision on sports.

I left Hillsboro after two years and went to another local school, Liberty High School. In a summer league game, we were trailing ten to zero in the bottom of the sixth. In Oregon, games are over after one team is ahead ten runs, and we needed a run to play another inning. In the bottom of the sixth, we had the bases loaded with no outs. My batter had a three-two count on him. The ball was in the dirt, and he swung and missed, and the catcher dropped the ball. Because first base was occupied with less than two outs, the batter was automatically out.

With the ball lying three feet in front of the plate, my runner on third (let's call him Albert Einstein) decided to break for home plate. He was tagged out by ten feet, out number two. While this was happening, my runner at second (let's call him Stephen Hawking) decided to go to third. He was thrown out by fifteen feet, out number three.

For the first time in baseball history, we had just struck out into a triple play. The home plate umpire, Tim Prosser, walked by me and had to put his hat over his face—he was laughing so hard (the guy was a friend of mine). I was beet red, my hat was sideways, and I was fuming. I told my team after that, that play would go down in history as the worst case of base running that has ever happened.

The next week, we had the bases loaded with no outs and hit an infield fly; and one of the kids, despite me yelling to get back, took off. He was easily tagged out. Another barely made it back, or it would have been another triple play. That team was clueless in running the bases.

I then went to Scappoose to be the head coach. Scappoose always had an excellent baseball program, and I felt honored to be the coach. We had a playoff game at Newport. We were down 5–4 in the top of the sixth. We had guys on first and second with 1 out. My number-two hitter was up. He was left-handed and very fast. I rolled the dice and had him bunt down the first baseline as he was struggling, and I wanted to make something happen. He laid down a perfect bunt. He was running right down the line. The pitcher picked up the ball and threw it. There was a collision at first; the ball went into right field, and we scored. When the play had ended, Ken Riley (the Newport coach) came out to talk to the umpire. Ken told me he was just throwing crap on the wall to see what stuck. The first-base umpire, Randy Knuths, started walking to home plate, never a good sign. After five minutes, he called my runner out and sent the runners back.

I did my best not to lose it as Randy was a guy I grew up with. Instead of being tied and the infield playing up, my number-three hitter grounded out, ending our season. I came to find out that the ball had hit my player in the shoulder. The worst part of this was that several of those kids would never play organized baseball again, being seniors. My principal was there and commended me for how I handled it. If the ump would have stayed out instead of interjecting himself, who knew what would have happened? Randy did call me the next day, and we talked about the call. When I officiated basketball, I always wanted the players to decide the game, not me.

In all the years I coached and the number of games I was involved in, my teams only made one triple play. We were playing against Central High School, which was one class higher than Scappoose. It was the bottom of the seventh, and the score was tied. They had the bases with no outs. Their batter hit a rocket-line drive up the middle. My shortstop, J. C. Gross, was positioned perfectly. He caught the ball, stepped on second, and threw to first. We won the game the next inning. It was a play where a miracle was needed, and we got one.

In the summer of my second year, we were scheduled to play Warrenton at the Seaside Tournament. Warrenton was coached by one of my ex-players, Lennie Wolfe. I told my team I did not care if we lost every other game that summer, but we damn well better win that one. We did win, and Lennie and I took some pictures after, although he never sent them to me. Earle Ramsey was my first ex-player that ever umpired one of my games. Jeff Moseman was the first one of my high school teammates who ever umpired one of my games.

We were playing an away game, and I had a player threaten another. I immediately took him out of the game. His dad came down and made threats. I called my athletic director. When we got back to Scappoose, I had the police there to make sure I got out of town safely. Sports are getting out of hand with the conduct. That is the one aspect that I do not miss.

My wife had applied and gotten a job at a hospital in San Diego. I informed the athletic director and principal that I would be resigning after the last game. We hosted a playoff game against Estacada and were beaten 5–4. It was a tough loss as we were leading 4–2 in the sixth. After the game, I told my players. It was tough as I had relationships with a lot of the kids. They had excelled that year. I was very lucky to coach this group. J. C. Gross and Jared Toman both got to play in the All-State game, the last time that Oregon ever had a 4A game.

CHAPTER 7

The Caddy Years

I started my life in the golf world as a cart man at the Creek on Long Island, New York. I worked my way up (or down) if you like as a starter and then a caddie because they made more money. We used to have large golf outings every week, and the caddies received large tips. I was also able to play every day and use the range. One night Peter Vicars, who was one of the assistant pros, invited me to play night golf. We bought glow-in-the-dark balls and played for about an hour until we both hit our balls into the Long Island Sound. When we returned to the main building, the head pro, John Sanges, was there. He said that Peter set off the alarm when we entered the building and told us not to do it again.

Peter was the first person I caddied for at a professional event. He was an absolute pleasure to be around with. He was a young man of about twenty-two and had a great future. I was devastated one night when a friend of mine called and said he had committed suicide. He was not doing well in school and decided to end his life. It was a tragedy. During my first year on tour, I wore his initials on my hat and prayed for him before every round. I miss him very much and was looking forward to the things he could have accomplished in his life.

As most of you who have played know, men like to relieve themselves on the course after drinking several adult beverages. At one of the more exclusive clubs on Long Island, they got a complaint from a woman member about it. They wrote back to her after a couple of weeks, and said, "After carefully researching your complaint, we have found it to be true. Therefore, we will be allowing women the same opportunities to urinate while playing."

I still laugh every time I think about this one.

We moved to Los Angeles, and I decided to try to caddie at the Riviera Country Club. I was hired and started to work my way up. This was shortly after the O. J. Simpson incident happened, so I heard all kinds of stories. We had a lot of events come in every week and got to play the course every Monday after the events. It was worth the drive I had to make every day. I was at the Riviera for about eight months, when my wife at the time got a job in Northern Virginia. I decided to go to the Congressional Country Club and try to caddie. It was extremely tough getting work there. Sometimes I would sit for six or seven hours without working, as it was all based on seniority. I decided that I wanted to try the professional circuit, so I looked at the LPGA schedule as I figured that would be easier than the PGA Tour.

I went to Myrtle Beach, South Carolina, trying to caddie my first LPGA event. I did not know then about working the parking lot. I showed up at the caddie tent very early and was the first one there. Shortly after I arrived, a burly-looking guy walked in. We started talking, and I found out that he was a local guy named Chip Wall. We waited several hours, and finally two players came in at the same time. I ended up working for Laurel Kean, and Chip worked for Kim Shipman. We played a practice round and got along great. Laurel shot well the first day. She birdied the first hole that I worked. The second day, she hit the ball off the fairway and hit a shot out of the rough. After hitting it, she was informed that it was an environmental area and was assessed a two-stroke penalty, the first in LPGA history. We ended up missing the cut, but I was hooked on being out there. I scheduled the Nashville Tournament for two weeks later, working again for Laurel. Chip ended up being my roommate for most of my years on tour.

I drove to Atlanta the next week and sat in the parking lot. I ended up working for Kim Williams for the week. We made the cut but did not finish very high. The weather was miserable, and the course was hilly and very hard to navigate. I also worked my first

Monday qualifier for Michelle Dobek. I did not do a very good job as I had not walked the course prior and was not much help to her. We became friends, and I worked for her later and did a much-better job.

I drove back to Sterling, Virginia, and flew to Nashville. We played a pro-am on Monday after I had walked the course early Monday morning. We played another pro-am on Thursday before the event. On Friday, Laurel shot a sixty-nine, three under. Saturday she shot seventy-two, so we had made the cut. On Sunday, we teed off semiearly. After shooting even par on the first nine, Laurel got hot on the back and shot a thirty. We were now at nine under for the event. After the round, she was going to load up her clubs. I told her no way. The leaderboard was crowded at ten under, with about six ladies there and nine holes to play. She went in and called her family and friends. I kept watching the board. Players kept dropping back. After ninety minutes, I told her we needed to go to the range just in case as there were only two ahead of us now.

It ended up being Laurel, Terri Jo Myers, and Nancy Harvey in a playoff. We played eighteen first, and everyone parred the hole. We went back to the par three, number seventeen next. Nancy hit her ball about thirty feet away, Laurel twenty feet, and Terri Jo about ten feet. Nancy went first and missed. Laurel looked at the putt and called me in for a read. She had not asked all week, and now I had to help with a potential 150,000 putt. The hardest thing about reading putts is how hard they are going to be hit. After talking, she hit hers and drained it. Terri Jo then made hers. Nancy was eliminated, and we played on. The third playoff hole was parred by both. We went back to seventeen. Laurel picked out the same club and teed up the ball. She called for me. I went to her, and she said, "Bring the bag." I made a comment that I did not want the other clubs to hear us talking about them. Everyone was laughing, and she had a huge smile. We both parred it again. Now to the fifth playoff hole.

We played eighteen again. Terri Jo parred the hole, and Laurel had a one footer to play another. It did an around the world and out; we had lost. I never changed my mood. I had kept her smiling and loose. She said that to the paper the next day. She was an absolute gem to work for. I have lots of stories that are very humorous over the course of my five years on Tour. That was as close as I would come to being on the winning bag, and it was amazing.

The year went by fast. Laurel kept her card, and I worked very hard to learn the courses and her tendencies. We were playing in a tournament in Atlantic City. Laurel had just bogeyed the sixteenth hole and was upset at herself because that had put us right on the cut line. We came up to the seventeenth hole. The course was very dry, and there was a reachable bunker in the middle. I said that a 3 wood was the right call. Laurel went ballistic and told me to never tell her what to hit. I knew she was mad at herself and not me but was taking it out on me. This went on for a minute. She finally took out the driver and blocked it right into another bunker. She let me have it all the way up the fairway. Once we were there, I walked into the distance and gave it to her. She was still upset.

After a few times, she asked what the distance was, and I gave it to her. She asked about the club, and we agreed. She took it out and hit to about six feet. She started walking. There was a marshal there that volunteered to rake the bunker. I said thanks, but I needed to let her cool down. He had heard everything, and I did not think he had ever heard anything like it. When I reached the green, Laurel had a huge smile. She said, "Great call."

I looked at her and smiled back and said the same phrase she had said many times to me coming up the fairway. She was laughing. She made birdie, and we made the cut. I learned very early how frustrating the game of golf is and that the player cannot blame themselves; too many bad things happened if they did. I was a big boy and could take anything they said because I knew it was not personal. I had great times working for Laurel. I could not have asked for a better person to be on the course with.

The year after Laurel lost her card, she was qualifying to play at Springfield, Illinois, in the Rail Tournament. I was working for Laurie Rinker Graham that week and had also worked the qualifier for another lady. Laurel shot a sixty-six and ended up in a three-way tie and forced into a playoff for one of the spots. Her caddie had left, and she asked me to carry for her. After three holes, she won the playoff. It was always so easy working for her. She won the tournament and became the first-ever LPGA player to win after Monday qualifying. It was also a State Farm bonus pool, and she received that after. I could not have been happier for her after all she had gone through in her career; it is so hard to win out there, and for the one weekend, she was the best on tour.

I was also lucky enough to work for many of the ladies, and every one of them does something different. It really is a tight-knit community, and you always root for people to do good. The money was not very good unless you finished in the top twenty every week. A lot of the ladies had to play the Monday qualifiers in order to pay their caddies for the week. Some of the ladies would use local caddies because they were less expensive than tour caddies. The parking lot was the place to hang out when looking for work.

Speaking of caddies, the pro golf world is chock-full of characters. Many of them have nicknames. They came from all walks of life and varying educations. For a lot of them, it was a week-to-week existence. Almost all of the caddies got paid the same except the ones working for the top players. We would get a percentage if we made the cut. A lot of times, caddies would borrow money. I never loaned anyone anything. There was one tournament when a friend of mine, John "White Shoes" Kenicke, was in the next-to-last group on Sunday. He had more caddies following his group than the final group had fans following it. They were all waiting after to accompany him to the finance tent when he cashed his check so he could pay them back. John rode with me once driving from one stop to the next. I let him drive so I could sleep for an hour. I woke up and we were going everywhere. I got back in the driver's seat. I found out later that he was legally blind.

I usually stayed with Chip Wall. He was a great roommate. Chip was retired Navy intelligence. He had some great stories but could not go into much detail because of security. Chip was easygoing and rarely had anything bad to say about anyone. There was one week in Corning, New York, that he worked for Kim Williams. Kim was a very demanding player to work for. After the first round, he came back to the room. His face was beet red, and every other word was a curse word. I said I was sorry but that I could not stop laughing. He made it through the week but said no more after that.

I stayed several times with Jeff "Tree" Cable and Jay Rothenberger. Jay used to keep the room so cold that you could hang meat in it. They are both great guys, and we became fast friends. Tree worked for Se Ri Pak and would tell us great stories about everything that he had to deal with and the media.

Jeff "Shadow" Jones was one of the true characters on tour. Shadow, or Shad as most of us called him, had his own set of terms that he used. "Down the road" meant missed the cut. The ballet was the local topless establishment. Church was the offtrack betting. One day when I was on the range with Laurel, Shad came up and said he went to church the night before. After he left, Laurel said that she did not know he was religious. I told her what it meant, and she cracked up laughing.

At one tour site, there was a small creek about two feet wide with a plank over it. Shadow fell into it. The next day one of the caddies put a sign next to it and called it "Shadow's Creek." Shad always wore a sweater in his room no matter where we were or what time of year it was. Shad was once fired by his player because she said she got a zit from him not cleaning his bag towel. He loved professional wrestling. Several times the WWF was in the same town, and we went. There was one time in Seattle that we went to the event. We had ringside seats. When the first match started, some kid came down and stood in front of us. I asked the kid if he would pay $25 to look at my butt. He said no.

I said, "Good, because I did not pay to look at yours." The policeman next to us removed him. Sadly, Shadow was involved in an auto accident driving from one event to another and lost his life. I will always treasure the times I spent with him.

On weeks that your players are off, many caddies would work for another player. It was a great way to meet people. One week I was working in Portland for Heather Daly Donofrio. Heather was a Yale graduate and extremely intelligent. She wanted very little information. Every player is different. Portland was a three-day tournament. We were on hole number seventeen the second day, right on the cut line with two holes to play. Most of the caddies knew what the cut line was going to be by watching the scoreboard. We decided on a club. Number seventeen had water up the right side. Heather hit a shot that leaked right and went into the water. It was not good. She asked, "What do you think?" and I said it was the right club. She hit it again, and it took two bounces and went it. We made the cut; it was an incredible turn of events.

I had a week off in South Carolina, so I decided to work for Ellie Gibson. Ellie had a reputation among the caddies as being extremely tough to work for. She had always been very friendly to me, so we started out right. On the fourth or fifth hole we were playing, I talked her into hitting a longer club out of the rough. The ball flew out, hit the front of the green, and went all the way through. She was very upset. I stopped as we were walking and told her that that one was my fault; I talked her into hitting it and she did nothing wrong. She said that in all her years no caddie had ever said anything like to her. I told her, "Let's get it up and down and make par." She did. It was a pleasure working for her, and I would have done it anytime.

I was working for Nancy Bowen during my last year on tour. There were some things going on at home that I needed to attend to and could no longer justify being on tour. I had to resign. Nancy was a joy to work for.

My friend Jeff King called me and asked if I could work two weeks on the Men's Tour for him at Torrey Pines and Riviera. I took the job and flew from Virginia. I would be working for Eric Booker. I met Eric on Monday morning after I had walked the south course. We played in a pro-am and worked well together. After the first three holes, he put his yardage book in the bag and said he did not need it because he knew what I was doing. After the round, he told me to be there at 7:00 a.m. the next day as we were playing a practice round with Tiger Woods.

I showed up at about 6:15 a.m. and cleaned the clubs, which is standard practice before, during, and after every round. At about 6:45 a.m., a large group of people came in by the putting green. We were on the tee at seven when Tiger came on. His caddie was his old college teammate, as Steve Williams had the weekend off. This was the first time he had played since he made a dramatic comeback on the back nine at Pebble Beach. Without hitting a practice ball, Tiger made a birdie on the first hole. He was easy to talk to and in a great mood. He is completely different than the person that you see on TV, but he has to be because it is his job to play for money. He told some jokes as we played. I had a nice time talking to his caddie. We had security inside and outside the ropes. The gallery was about fifty to seventy-five people that early in the morning. I will always be a Tiger fan; he was class the entire round.

We made the cut at Torrey Pines. After the players got their scorecards, Eric handed them to me to keep. I asked him when he liked it back after the hole, and he said he didn't; I would be keeping it. On the Ladies Tour, the caddies never keep the card. It was a compliment to me, and I was very happy to do it although there was a lot of pressure, knowing that you better not make a mistake. The next week, we went to Los Angeles. It was nice coming back to a course that I knew well. The wind usually started blowing around 11:00 a.m. from the ocean and picked up during the day. Riviera is also divided by barranca, and the ball breaks differently on every part of the course. We were on the cut line the second day and made the turn to play number one; we had started on number ten. Eric hit one left, and we made double. We ended up missing the cut, but it was an incredible experience for me. I appreciated Jeff asking and Eric letting me work for him.

After that week, I worked a couple more LPGA events and called it a day. I had a great five years on tour.

I needed to find work during my last year living in Virginia. Lowes Island Country Club was a few blocks away from my house, and they were hiring starters. I applied, and after a complete background check, I was hired. I found out why they needed background checks after working there for a few days. There were many high-profile people and politicians that were members there. One particular Sunday, one of the high-profile members was scheduled to play on a Sunday with his wife. When he came to the first tee, I addressed him as Mister (I will not put his name here because I will not violate his privacy), and he said, "Mike, my name is ____, and please call me that." He was one of the nicest guys at the club. It was entertaining to turn on the TV the next day and see him.

My divorce was finalized, and I decided to move back to Portland.

CHAPTER 8

The High School Referee Years

When I was a sophomore at Lewis & Clark College, my coach Mickey Hergert had a basketball-officiating course. Several of my friends and I took the class. Mickey was an outstanding high school and college official. I learned a lot. We would work city-league games in Lake Oswego for $5 a game, which came in handy to a college kid. Most city-league players are ex-high-school or college players who have lost a step (or two) and still think they should be in the NBA. We had contests during the games about who could go the longest without blowing a whistle, who could blow it the fastest, etc. It was very entertaining to us but not to the players. We usually had to call a lot of technicals because of the language the players used.

I decided to join the Portland Basketball Officials Association in my junior year. First-year officials would work CYO, junior high, and lower-level high-school games. I got to see a lot of very bad basketball. I was fortunate because I had already had a year of experience, and Coach Hergert had taught me well. My first game was a ninth-grade game at the old Jackson High School. I was always told to show up early. I arrived at 2:30 p.m. for a 4:00 p.m. game. One Sunday, I was officiating a sixth-grade CYO game on a Saturday at Cathedral Catholic school in Portland with my partner Earl Wong. The fans were very unruly. In the second half, my partner had enough. He cleared the gym. This was a great idea, except for one thing. All of these kids were driven to the game by the parents who had just been ejected. They were all waiting in the parking lot. The police had to be called to break it up. This was the first time that ever happened to me; the second time will be later down the story.

The PBOA had many characters who worked games from all walks of life. My first commissioner was Jerry Laurens. Howard Mayo was the president. The next year, Howard became commissioner. Howard was a by-the-book official who taught mechanics and the rules. There was no gray area. I moved up fast as my judgment was good, and I always worked hard. I was voted in as a regular member after my third year and was able to work varsity games. I was still learning a lot. We used to do girls' JV and varsity games on the same night. It paid $20 for both, but the basketball was really bad. Most teams would have one girl who was decent, the rest learning how to play. The games took forever.

Now for some stories. Estacada was very tough to work. The small outlying towns from Portland were extremely vocal during games, especially on a Friday as there was nothing to do except go to the games. On this particular night, one of our officials was working their game. The fans were really bad. At halftime, this ref went into his bag that was at the scorer's table and pulled out a gun and said to all the fans, "Anyone want to yell at me now?" Needless to say, the police arrived, he was arrested, and he never worked another game.

We used to work in a small logging town named Vernonia. The usual practice was to arrive early and park behind the gym, backing your car into the spot. At halftime, you would take your bag and possessions and put them into your car. You would leave the car keys in your game jacket. When the game was over, you would run to the bench, grab your keys, and run out the back. It was a mad dash out of town trying to beat the locals. This happened on more than one occasion.

My first ejection happened at a sophomore game at Aloha High School. I had to issue a technical foul to the Jesuit coach in the first quarter for his behavior. As a young official, the older coaches would try to intimidate the officials. In the second quarter, I was taking the ball out of bounds under the basket, and I looked to see the coach standing next to me yelling—technical number two. Back then, three were required for ejection.

In the fourth quarter, I made a call, and he broke his clipboard over the bench in anger. He got number three and was ejected. He had no assistant. I asked if anyone that worked at the school was there. The bus driver said he did, but I told him he was not a staff member. The game was forfeited to Aloha. Needless to say, I was called every name under the sun as we walked off the floor. When a coach is ejected the Oregon Schools become involved. I had to write a report as did the coach, and then they investigated. Their coach made up some nonsense including his statement that "he gently discarded his clipboard." Fortunately, the Aloha athletic director and Commissioner Mayo stood behind me. My call was justified.

I was working a game at LaSalle High School between them and the Stayton Eagles. This was the second game they had played that was very late in the season. They were ranked #1 and #2. LaSalle's gym was called "the brick oven" because it is small and always hot. The game was on a Friday night and was sold out. It was a very close game and tied with roughly forty seconds left. LaSalle had the ball and was holding it for one last shot. The Stayton player got within five feet, and I counted to five and called a jump ball for him being closely defended. We had to jump the ball back then. Stayton won the tip and then won the ball at the end of the game. Both teams had Oregon legends coaching them. LaSalle's coach was Jack Cleghorn. Even though the call went against him, he always treated me with class after the incident. I learned a very valuable lesson that night that I always took with me: try your best to let the kids decide the game. Even though according to the rule book it was the correct call, it was a horrid call on my part and the single worst call I ever made. My officiating partner Gary Nikkari and I discussed it after, and he told me those important words. It was the last time that it ever happened.

Tigard hired a new basketball coach from California. He came in and was causing all kinds of problems for officials. It was so bad that Howard Mayo had to go to a couple of their games and sit behind the bench. I had a sophomore game at Tigard on a Thursday night. Everything went well, except for a jerk sitting behind the bench constantly yelling at me and my partner. I finally threw him out in the third quarter. It was this coach. Little did he know, I had their varsity game the next night. I wish I would have had a camera when he saw that it was me working the game. He got a technical very early and said nothing more.

When I started working in the World Basketball League, they would give us Converse shoes. They had a white star and chevron on them. Howard used to call them skunk shoes. I also did not wear a lanyard as it slowed me down making the calls. Howard would always give me a bad time whenever he showed up at one of my games. I truly loved the man and what he stood for.

I was gone from the PBOA for many years. When I returned to Portland, I decided to work again. I had to work on a few lower-level games before I could do the varsity games again. That did not take long. During my return year, I had five ejections. Two were from a fight, the other three from coaches. I rarely heard anything from the side; if I did, there was going to be a problem.

We were required to wear contacts in all pro basketball games. I always wore my glasses in and then out because I looked different. I was working a game one night, and one of the players coached had a sister playing in the game. Her mom did not recognize me until halftime. Another time I went to get some dinner after a game. The people in front of me were talking about the game. I said, "Those refs were sure lousy tonight." The lady in front agreed, not knowing I was one of them. I laughed all the way home.

During one Christmas season, I was working a game at a small high school. My partner made a questionable call and was getting yelled at. That coach called time. I told my partner that I would handle the time-out to keep him away from the bench. When the time-out was over, the coach started again. I told him I had heard enough. I finally gave him a technical, and he went berserk. He did not stop and got another, ejecting him. I told the timer to set the clock to thirty seconds for him to leave. He finally went to the door and stood there, still yelling. I told him he had to leave the premises, and he started yelling again. I could have forfeited the game because he refused to leave, but the athletic director from the home school escorted him out, and I let the OSSA deal with him.

One of my favorite partners was Dan Loftus. I played against Dan when he was in high school at North Salem. We worked many games together, and Dan was always smiling. I loved pranking him on the floor, and he never knew it was me. We had a big game at Beaverton on a Friday. Their student-body section was extremely vocal. Dan went over to the scorer's bench about ten minutes before the game started. I went to the center of the student-body section and asked who was in charge. A boy said he was. I told him that my partner's name was Dan, and he loved to hear them calling his name. They were all over Dan during the game.

At halftime, Dan asked me if I had heard them calling his name and wondered how they knew. I said yes and that they probably hear it when they announced his name. I was laughing under my breath. Dan and I had a game at Lakeridge High School during the Christmas season. Dan made a questionable call and the visiting team called a time-out. I was by their bench. After the time-out, I went over and told their players that it was his first-ever varsity game, and he was very nervous. The players kept telling him the rest of the game that he was doing a great job for the first time, and Dan said he did not understand why. Sadly, Dan passed away from COVID-19 in 2021. The world lost one of its best people, and he is truly missed.

I was working a Westview vs. Lakeridge game one night. Westview had a six-foot-nine center named Landon Lucas. I was never a fan of three seconds: I called it the same way that I did in the pros, 2.9 seconds without the ball in the key, another 2.9 seconds if the ball came in. If the player passed the ball out after that, it was an immediate three-second call. Lucas was in for 2.9, got the ball, and slammed it home—no call. We went to the other end. Lakeridge held the ball for five seconds, and I called it. The ball went back to Westview. Lakeridge's coach was Dane Walker. Dane was an outstanding coach, but also being a baseball coach, he was very vocal. He was not happy. We went to the other end, and once again Lucas was in the key for 2.9 seconds, got the ball, and slammed it home.

Walker had seen enough. He yelled at me, "So you can count to five but not to three?"

I said, "I can also count to two" and assessed a technical foul on him. The fans enjoyed it, although Coach Walker did not. I had him many times after that, and not once did he ever yell. He was a class act, and I did enjoy working his games.

I always worked a lot of games for Howard Mayo. He knew he could call me anytime, and I would be there. In all of my years officiating, I was never late and did not miss any games. There were a few times that the envelope was pushed as Howard used to like to have us work an early game and then drive to a varsity game. The closest I ever came was a Friday night when I had to drive from Southridge in Beaverton to St. Helens. I made it by fifteen minutes. One Saturday, I worked two sixth grades in the morning. Since I had worked two games the prior day, I put all my clothes in the wash when I came home. Two hours after I had gotten home, Howard called. He needed someone immediately at the Waldorf Academy. It was about a twenty-minute drive from my home. I told him I would but that my pants and shirts were in the wash. He asked if I had black sweatpants. I said yes. I had an old shirt. He told me to wear those. I showed up and worked the game; it was the only time in history that he ever approved of anyone working a game in an unapproved uniform.

I was working a high school playoff game with Anthony Henderson a few years ago. The game was at Parkrose against Hood River Valley. The game started, and there was a guy sitting on the end of the HRV bench chirping at us. During a time-out in the second quarter, I had enough and walked over to the bench. I asked him what his job description was. He told me he was the trainer. I told him not anymore. He said he could say what he wanted; I said not anymore. I told him to go twenty rows up into the crowd, and if the team needed him, he could come back down temporarily. But until then, he was not sitting on the bench.

The coach came down and said, "He is my trainer."

I told the coach, "Not anymore" and told him what had happened. I told him I was saving his team from getting a T because that was going to be the next step. It was a big game for both teams, and

I did not want to have to call something that might decide it. There were no problems after that.

I loved working Special Olympics games. The kids played with heart, and the final score never really mattered. Being a huge soccer fan, I always loved watching players exchange shirts after the game was over. I had so many old shirts, that I decided to do this with the kids who played. It was amazing to see the looks on their faces when I gave them my shirt. I had one mother bring her son up to me and tell me her son had my shirt. I said yes he did because I gave it to him. She was almost in tears. I was just glad to be a part of it.

I was at Wilsonville one year for a pre-Christmas tournament game. The game was a blowout. At the start of the quarter, one of the Wilsonville coaches asked if he could ask me a question, and I said absolutely. I do not remember what he asked, but after it was over, the head coach Chris Roche asked me. With a straight face, I said, "Chris, you are not going to believe it, your coach asked me if I could throw him out because he needed to finish Christmas shopping."

Roche was cracking up laughing, and the assistant turned red. I always tried to keep a good relationship, and with some coaches, it was much easier than others. Being a coach myself, I always understood where they were coming from.

I wish I would have been miked up during my last year of working high school. One night I was working a varsity game. In the first minute, I made a call against the home team. As I was walking by, the coach said, "That call was terrible."

I stopped walking to the bench, turned around, and said, "If you are talking to me, that is the last time that is happening. I have known you for ten minutes, and this relationship is not starting out well for you. If you say anything else, the last thing anyone here will see is you walking out the door."

He never said another word and went out of his way after the game to say thank you.

On another night, I was working a game. During the third quarter, the coach called a time-out and asked if he could talk to me. I said of course. I was always willing to talk to any coach; I just would not listen to complaints. He went on for forty-five seconds about the call. Finally, he said, "What do you think?"

I told him I thought he had very good skills at explaining, but his listening skills were not good because the time-out was over, and we had to play. Every one of the parents behind his or her bench was laughing. He sat down and said nothing for the rest of the night.

In my last year of officiating, I had not called three seconds the entire year going into my last two games before I retired. I was working at Central Catholic, and we were in the second half. I finally called it. During the next time-out, I went over to the Central bench. After they broke to come out on the floor, I told their coach I was pissed at him. He asked why. I said I had gone all year without calling a three, and his kid blew it. I told him I counted to ten and after telling him to get out, he still stood there clueless. The coach could not stop laughing.

I have worked thousands of games with hundreds of partners. When we put that striped (or solid in some cases) shirt on, we become one. Race, religion, political beliefs, sexual orientation, and everything else were tossed out the window. I have worked with people just starting all the way up to the best in the profession. I have never considered myself better than anyone I have worked with. I will admit that there were nights that I knew I had to cover a little more on the court to help out my partner. I will also admit that the higher you climb, you had better have a big ego in the fact that you know are good, or you would not be there.

You also better be able to get yelled at on *every* call every time down the floor. Youth and high school officials do it for the most part for love of the game. I always said that the day that I could not give 100 percent was the day I retired. It never mattered to me what the level of the game was. I would obviously let more go at the lower levels, but that did not stop me from busting my butt working. Every kid who plays deserves that from all officials.

When you walk into the gym or outside court to work a game, you are walking into an area where many times your only friend is the person or persons you are working with. I can sincerely say that in all the games I worked, there was only one time when I was truly pissed at my partner. It happened in Canada, and there was a full-scale brawl. My partner did nothing to help, and he was fired the next day by the league office when they reviewed the game.

One thing every official needs to understand (and this is coming from someone who was a baseball coach) is when you walk in, you are only there for approximately ninety minutes. You have not been to the practices, rode the bus to the game, had to deal with parents, had to teach class, etc. We really have no idea what is going on behind the scenes, which leads me to parents. As an official, you tolerate what you want to. The first thing I learned at NBA camp was that if someone pisses you off, you T or toss them. I have called more Ts than probably one hundred officials combined. I have ejected more than probably five hundred combined. I have thrown players, coaches, fans, parents, and even a mascot.

As a coach, I asked for three things: consistency, hustle, and knowledge of the rules. Umpires that did those rarely had a problem with me. There are several people here that I officiated with and have had officiate my games. I respect them all. I can tell you as a coach, how you present yourself will immediately tell me what I am getting. I could usually tell within ten minutes after watching umpires I had never seen work. I can tell you as an official and as a coach, once the game is over, it is forgotten. One of my friends on here was umpiring a game. He made a couple of calls that were questionable, and I was chirping at him from the dugout. He put me on a bench suspension, which I fully deserved. After the game, he was standing in the parking lot with his partner. I went over and told him good job. He was surprised as he thought I was mad at him. I told him, game over, it ends there. I think as soon as an official understands this, you really get to the next level.

It goes a long ways as an official to show up early. The last thing a coach or athletic director needs is the worry that the officials are not there. They have a lot more to do than having to see where the refs are.

Lastly, the best part of working the games for me was the friendship and times spent with—and getting to know—my partners. I have so many stories, and those are being put to paper. The last game

I worked was at Hillsboro High School. This was with a week left in the season. I told Steve Scott that my career ends there as they had a couple of players who had played for me in baseball, and the athletic director, Steve Drake, was a friend of mine. They were also playing Putnam, and their coach Gregg Griffin and I went back to our college days. I wanted to go out on my terms. At halftime, I signed my referee jacket and gave it to Gary Walker, who was keeping score. After the game, I gave my shirt to one of the kids, another shirt to another one, and finally my whistle and a PBOA undershirt to another. I have never looked back.

Since I returned to Oregon in the summer of 2021, I started officiating again. It took a couple of weeks to get the legs working again. I worked about forty games, and two ejections and a lot of technicals later, I finished the summer.

I was invited to go to Everett, Washington, to be one of the referee supervisors for the tournament. Because of a shortage of officials, I ended up working thirteen games. I can officially say that in all the years I have worked, this was the most enjoyable. I had all men's games. I had zero problems, and most of the players shook my hand after. I was even given a gift by a player—a nice case for my glasses (I was out of contacts, so I had to wear my glasses). I sent a letter to the mayor of Everett complimenting their city and people. She answered back immediately. Everett is one place I will always go to.

My stories will now continue about basketball as I am working high school games again.

During my sixth or seventh year in the PBOA, I was invited to a PAC 8 officials tryout in Eugene at the University of Oregon. I had not done three-man mechanics before, so I would be learning on the fly. The tryout went well, but at that time, officials had to choose between college or professional. I wanted to go professional. I looked for the best way to get there. One of the NBA officials named Paul Mihalek was having a camp in Tampa, Florida. I flew across the country to attend. After the camp was over, I won the best official trophy, and my career was off.

In less than a month I received a call from Seattle, and they invited me to come up and officiate a large NBA pro-am tournament. It went very well. The next summer, I decided to attend Hue Hollins's NBA officials camp in Inglewood. The camp had a large number of attendees. I did not know anyone but worked very hard. One day I was working a game, and the NBA chief of officials Darrel Garretson came in. He came over and talked to me after my stint on the court, and I was pumped. I was selected to work the eight o'clock NBA Summer League at Inglewood High School.

While my partner and I were getting dressed, Al Lewis (Grandpa Munster) came into the bathroom. We had to change in the public restroom for the games. Al was a massive basketball fan and especially a UCLA fan and would attend their players' games. There were a couple of UCLA players in the game. Al said hello and shook our hands. Al then went to the urinal, and when he was finished he walked right out, bypassing the sink. My partner and I both laughed and were happy we shook his hand before, not after. The game went well, and I was very happy I attended.

In the fall, I was invited to work some of the Portland Trailblazers' fall camps. I was nervous at first until we started working them. My partner told me that when we were working, one of us would watch Maurice Lucas, and the other official would watch the other nine guys. Lucas was extremely intelligent, and he always knew where the officials were.

My officiating friend Kevin Backlund called and we were offered to work the Seattle SuperSonics preseason camp. We would work three minutes of scrimmages every night, and on the last night, they would play a full-game scrimmage in front of fans. They played in Lacey, Washington, at St. Martin's College. The game was sold out. The players were great to both of us, and Coach Bernie Bickerstaff could not have treated us any nicer.

When I returned home, I was invited to work the NBA Pro-Am Winter league in Seattle. I would drive up early Saturday morning and work two games Saturday and Sunday and then drive home. I rarely got any nonsense from the players because a lot of them had seen me work the Sonics games, and credibility goes a very long way in the games. The game fees paid for gas and a little more, but I was not doing it to make money. I returned again to Hue's camp the next year to work on things that I needed to address.

During the spring, I received a call from Norm Drucker. I will discuss Norm a little later. They were starting up a league for six-foot-five players and under called the World Basketball League. The WBL was started by NBA legend Bob Cousy's idea. The tryouts would be in Vancouver, British Columbia. I drove the five-hour trip from Oregon, not knowing what to expect. I worked about ten minutes of the game, and then Norm talked to me. I said I was hired and would be working mostly the Vancouver teams' home games that were played at BC Place.

I worked opening night in Vancouver and had no problems. The second or third night up, that all changed. Vancouver had signed a guy named Andre Patterson, who had been listed as six foot eight in college and was appropriately named Andre the Giant. He had been kicked out of the Continental Basketball Association for conduct. They were playing Calgary, and one of their players was driving to the basket when Patterson sucker punched him in the stomach. I was under the basket and saw everything. The Calgary player returned punches, and a third player from Calgary joined in the beating. Both benches cleared, and with the help of the coaches, the fight was finally broken up. I had been on the floor trying to pull the players off, and when I got up, I had gum and popcorn on me as the fight had gone into the stands. I looked up, and my partner was standing at half court, doing nothing. I was pissed that he had not helped me. I walked out and asked WTF he was doing. He said he would handle everything. I told him to piss off, and I was taking care of it; I was the lead that night, which meant I was the crew chief. I threw out all three involved and called my supervisor after the game. That was the last game that that official ever worked as he was let go. The league looked at the tape and levied fines to those who left the bench. Toward the end of the first year, I was sent to Calgary to work. It was the first time flying to a game and was thoroughly enjoyable.

While I was home, I used to work the NBA Pro-Am Games at Irving Park in Portland. Darrel Garretson was in town for an NBA Clinic, and I asked him to come over and observe. He came to a game and was there for about fifteen minutes. I called him the next day, and he let me have it for gaining ten pounds. My NBA dreams were over, so I moved on.

In the fall, I was invited back for the Sonics preseason camp at Seattle U. The last day of camp was the game. In the second quarter, we were shooting a free throw. In those days, we only had two officials. The guy on the baseline is the lead; the guy outside is the trail. I was under the basket and would administer the second free throw by bouncing the ball back to the shooter. As I stood next to the Sonics player who was six feet ten and weighed about 250 pounds (I will not post his name because I would never want this to get back to him), he said to me, "Back off please, I had something for lunch that did not agree with me."

I said thank you, grabbed the ball, bounced the ball back to the player, and moved as far down the line as I could. He let one fly. I could see the press sitting under the basket holding their noses. I got out of there fast.

We then went to the other end; I was the trail and my partner was now the lead. Now I knew that if I did not call something, I would be headed back into the gaseous fog now hanging on the other end. I called a cheap shooting foul, and whenever that happens, the referees switch positions. Now the fun began: the team went down the court, and my partner ran right into it. I could see him trying to hold his breath. I could hardly contain myself from laughing. Finally, one of the teams called a time-out. He came up and said it was the worst thing he had ever smelled. I told him what I did, and he kept calling me a-hole the rest of the game.

In the second year, I traveled equally between Vancouver, Calgary, and Las Vegas. I used to work two games at one site and then a couple at the next. When we flew into Canada, we had to make up an excuse why were there because they had a problem if we were doing something that a Canadian citizen could do. Most of us said we had girlfriends up there. We always had to take our game uniform with us in the cabin, so that the bags would not get lost. We usually traveled on the first flight in the morning in case of delays.

I was chosen to work the league All-Star Game in Las Vegas. This was a huge award. I would be working with ex-NBA official Ken Faulkner, and the game was nationally televised on sports channels in the US. Norm Drucker made the trip. Working in Las Vegas was great because Jerry Tarkanian came to the games and always sat courtside. He was always nice to talk to.

A little about Mr. Drucker. Norm was from New York and had a heavy accent. He could deadpan a line like no one else. He was also the only referee to ever toss Wilt Chamberlain from a game. Norm was the director of officials for the World Basketball League. I spent a lot of time with Norm, picking his brain. He told me one of the greatest stories of all time. Bill Russell, who played for the Boston Celtics and is still making commercials, does not sign autographs. Mr. Russell has a deal with the credit card companies that he does not sign. Norm asked him a couple of times for an autograph. After one game, to his surprise, Bill gave him an autographed ball. Norm was so excited that he came home and gave it to his son. Norm went away on another road trip and came home to find his son playing with the ball in the front yard, shooting baskets. Classic!

The day before the All-Star Game, Norm had gotten tickets for all three of us to see Tom Jones. We were sitting and waiting for the show to start, and a guy came by to take pictures. He asked what we were doing there, and Norm said with a straight face, "We are homosexuals from San Francisco here for the weekend." I spit out my water. Ken was red from laughing. It was the funniest thing I had ever heard. Norm said it all with a straight face.

The game went well. The final score was 148 to 144. It was nonstop up and down the floor, and we got excellent ratings. Later that summer, the Portland Trailblazers played the Utah Jazz at Civic Stadium in Portland. The NBA cleared it so that I could work the game with NBA official Terry Durham and another of my friends, Monte Bousquet. There were approximately twenty-four thousand people in attendance, and it was the largest crowd I had ever worked in front of. I was on the front page of the Oregonian sports page the next day, throwing the opening jump ball.

The World Basketball had some interesting coaches. They were all outstanding coaches with great basketball knowledge, or they would not have been hired to coach in the league. Some of them concentrated on coaching and left their assistants to ride us. Others spent most of the night telling us how the game should be called. That brings me to a coach named Mike Frink. Mike was the coach for the Vancouver Nighthawks the first year. Coach Frink was, and is, an outstanding coach, and his résumé is second to none. For whatever reason, I gave Mike more technical fouls than anyone else in my career.

One night, I went into the press area before the game to get a bottle of water. I always wear my glasses to and after the game, as I look different. I heard Coach Fink ask someone who the officials were for that game, and when he was told I was one of them, I heard him say, "Oh shit." I went out laughing.

After the second year, I was working the Seattle SuperSonics' preseason game. Mike was there and came over to talk to me. He apologized for everything in the past and said he had just been hired in Saskatoon as the new head coach and told me things would be different. I said I was looking forward to it. In the second quarter of the first game the next year, I had to issue a technical against him. I never took it personally as I knew he was only doing his job.

There was one night in Calgary when my partner and I had a rough game. The last thing an official wants to see is his name in the paper as it means there was trouble in the game. We always took the first plane out of town the next morning. I got to the airport an hour before the flight and noticed Coach Frink and his players. Since I was going to where they were, I knew we were on the same flight. This had happened before as we usually stayed in the same hotel. The players were always great and never said a word about any game. I went to the counter and asked to sit as close to the front as I could. I sat right behind first class and was by myself. I boarded the plane last. I was hoping no one saw me. About ten minutes into the flight, Coach Frink walked up and asked if he could talk to me. I said of course, as he was acting like a gentleman. We had a nice conversation, and then he took out the scorebook. He explained that the other team scored

40 percent (or more) of their points on free throws. After a couple of other minutes about stats, he asked me what I thought. I told him to stop having his team commit fouls to stop the clock, and then we would not have to call them. He just shook his head. I did admire the fact that he acted professionally.

One last thing about the coach, ne never wore socks. I can still remember the fans chanting, "Coach needs socks." It always made me smile. He is now coaching college basketball, and I wish him nothing but the best.

One thing officiating in the WBL was for certain, you were going to hear it from both benches all night long. It was only a matter of how much you were willing to take. Hue Hollins had taught me several things. One of them was when you get pissed off, you give them a technical. I call a lot and had many ejections during my first two years. At the start of my third year, fellow official Mike Eggers, who I worked a lot with, asked if he could tell me something. I said absolutely. He told me that the players and coaches had gotten the message from me and that I should ease up a bit. I thanked him and did just that, as I always respected his opinion. My technical fouls and ejections decreased dramatically.

We usually took a taxi from the hotel to the games at Thomas & Mack. We were on a strict time schedule when we had to be at the arena. Neal Kay was another ex-NBA official. He came out of Bally's with his partner, and it was pouring rain. When that happens, the queues back up. This time they were really long. It would have been at least a thirty-minute wait. The Domino's guy was just walking out, and Neal yelled at him, "Domino's delivers, right?"

The guy said, "You bet."

He told him to get them to the arena (a five- to ten-minute drive), and he would take care of him. He gave him $20; it was his best tip of the day. The security guys were cracking up seeing two referees get out of the Domino's truck.

In the third year, I was traveling all over the United States and Canada. I had one stretch where I had the national TV game of the week, three Saturdays in a row. On a Sunday, we had a national TV game scheduled for a 7:00 p.m. start. We all had game-day routines.

Mine was to go to a mall and walk from 10:00 a.m. to 12:00 p.m. and get lunch there. I would then sleep from 12:30 p.m. to 2:30 p.m. Night games were rough because we usually ate after and got home past midnight. If we were traveling, we had to be at the airport early because we always flew on the first plane in the morning.

Back to the story. I did my walk and went back to go to sleep. At 1:00 p.m. I got a call. It was from the Las Vegas team asking where we were. They said it was a 2:00 p.m. game. We were never notified. I told them we were on the way. I called my partner, and we ran down to the lobby. We were both wearing T-shirts and flip-flops. We had rules about what we were allowed to wear to games, and those were not one of them. It did not matter. We got to the arena at 1:35 p.m., threw on our uniforms, and made it onto the court fifteen minutes prior to the game, which was the rule. I will never forget getting to taste my lunch as I never ate that close to a game. After that, I always went two hours early before tip-off. I loved the big arenas where I could run underneath them.

During the middle of my third year, Terry Durham asked me to officiate a game at Portland Community College between the Blazers and Team USA. It was never mentioned in the media until after the game because they wanted no one there. Team USA was loaded. They had Alonzo Mourning, Todd Day, Kenny Anderson, and a lot more. Coach K was the head guy. PJ Carlisimo and Joe Boeheim were his assistants. Earl Strom used to love to make a bad call against the home team very early in the game to get the fans involved. The year after Earl retired from the NBA, he was in Portland trying to get a job on the radio with Bill Schonley. Earl was sitting courtside with Schonley. The game started, and Coach K started chirping relentlessly about everything.

When the first time-out came, Terry and I met at the center circle. He said, "If this would have been a regular-season game, he would have given him a technical."

I said, "If this were a regular-season game, I would have run him."

In the second quarter, we had a time-out, and I was standing by the table at center court. I always talked to everyone and turned and said, "Earl, I took less shit from my ex-wife than I am now."

Strom and Schonley laughed for five minutes. We finally finished the game.

The next day, I had to fly out to work a game in Calgary. I used to park my car at the Marriott and ride the shuttle for free. When I walked into the lobby, Earl was there. He immediately asked if I had any time as I told him where I was going. Since I always go three to four hours early, I said absolutely. He told me he was still laughing from the day before, and it was one of the best lines he had ever heard. We talked for about an hour before I had to go. *I could not pass up the opportunity to talk to a referee legend.* Just to be able to spend an hour with this man was every official's dream. Earl never got the job and passed away in 1994. He was sixty-six when he passed from a brain tumor.

Back in the nineties, most of the teams in the World Basketball League had mascots, guys dressed as characters. On this particular night, the mascot from one of the teams decided to talk trash every time I was under the basket. Finally, I had enough and ejected him. He said, "You cannot do that."

I told him, "Just because you are dressed like a bird does not give you the right to be an idiot."

He was still yelling as the police escorted him out of the building. I had to write it up on my after-game report, and Norm Drucker laughed.

At the start of the fifth year, the league expanded again. I was lucky enough to referee opening night in Winnipeg in 1992 before a sold-out crowd. Burton Cummings (The Guess Who) came into our dressing room before the game and spent some time with us. He is a true gentleman and one of my best World Basketball League memories. He then went out and did stunning versions of both anthems.

I was working NBA Summer League games when I was home. Back then, a lot of NBA players would show up and play. I was working one game with Greg Willard. One of the coaches was acting like a fool. I finally tossed him before the half, and we had no problems after that. When the game was over, he was beating on our dressing-room door. Greg asked me if I would like him to handle it, and I said thanks, but he wanted me. The coach was swearing profusely. I told him that he had his say on the court and that he was now on my personal time. I told him to stop acting like a jerk. The guy walked away. When we walked out, he was standing there. He held out his hand and apologized. I shook his hand and told him I respected that. When the game was over, I left it on the floor. Sadly, Greg passed away a couple of years ago. He was an outstanding official and an even better person. The world lost a great one when he passed.

In the fifth year of the league, it was in trouble financially. They had paid for our flights and hotels but not our per diem and game fees for a month. We kept getting promised that the pay would be there. It was a Saturday night in August, and I was in Saskatoon for a game against Calgary. In pro basketball, you never talk to the coaches before a game; you only talk to the captains. The coaches already know who you are, and they will tell you that every time up and down the floor, no matter what call from both benches.

I have been asked what is said during those captain meetings. Many times we had been told by Norm what teams had been getting away with and to look out for it. Sometimes we would say something to avoid a bad scene. Most times I would say hello to them and ask if they had any questions about any calls in games from the prior week.

This night was different. I had called the head of our officials, as my partner and I were both thinking about not working because of pay. He assured us that we would. Before the game, when we met with the captains, I asked both if they had been paid. They both said yes. I told them that we had not, and I was taking zero nonsense from anyone. They both said no problem. I had worked enough of their games, and they knew me and knew I was not the one to BS them. By midway through the second quarter, I had ejected both of the coaches.

In the third quarter, the Calgary captain, Chip Engelland (who is now an assistant coach with the San Antonio Spurs) came up and told me that this was the best game they had in five years with the coach. He said I should have done it long ago. Chip and I had a history. I once threw him out of a forty-point blowout that they were ahead. He had shot a three and was fouled, but I did not call it. He let me have it, and I gave him some rope before it was too much. He was as fierce a competitor as anyone I had ever seen as well as the best three-point shooter in our league. After that night we never had another problem. I am glad to see him coaching as he went to Duke, and his basketball IQ was off the wall.

Back to the story. The game ended with no problems, and I flew back to Los Angeles the next morning. I opened the *LA Times,* and the first thing I saw was that the league had folded. I had worked the last game. The money man for the league was Phar-Mor executive Mickey Monus, who eventually went to jail because of this, and Phar-Mor went bankrupt. By the way, the $3,000 they owe me will never be seen, as all the officials were written off during the bankruptcy.

I worked one more NBA Summer League and knew that I was not going to ever work there. I did get a call one year because the regular officials were going out on strike, but I told them no because I would not work a game with the guys who taught me everything standing outside. I took many years off until I moved back to Portland and started working high school games again.

CHAPTER 9

The San Diego Years: 2019 to Present

After moving to San Diego, I decided that I needed to do something instead of being at home all the time. I applied for a head-coaching job at Francis Parker School. Parker is an exclusive private school about five miles from my house. To my surprise (since I had no connections of any kind in San Diego), I was called in for an interview. The interview went very well in my opinion, but having been through many of these before, you never really know how it went. Time passed and no word, never a good sign. After about three weeks, the athletic director, Anthony Thomas, called me. He told me that they hired another man but wanted to know if I would be interested in coaching the JV team. At this point in my career, I told him I would love to. I scheduled an appointment to meet the man they hired, Amad Stephens. I met Amad and he was easy to talk to, and we both had the same ideas about coaching. I was hired.

The JV team was made up of a lot of freshmen and several kids who had never played before. Parker had a no-cut policy. I knew right away that this would be a long year. I had no catcher, so I had to take volunteers. The young man who volunteered was an actor. I told him that this would be his greatest role. He did the absolute very best that he could. I had two guys who could pitch, but we always struggled to score runs. After losing our first three games, we were scheduled against Chula Vista. Chula Vista was very comparable to my crew. I managed like there was no tomorrow. We ended up winning 5–4 but something felt very different about this one. When I got home, I had a call from Oregon that my friend and mentor Jerry Gatto had passed away earlier in the evening. Call it whatever you like, but I know Jerry's spirit was there with me. I could never explain it. That was the only game we won that year. I tried to make the season as fun as I could for the kids because I knew that for most of them, it was going to be the only time they played organized baseball.

Amad ran the Garciaparra Baseball travel teams in San Diego. He invited me to help coach. The talent level of the kids was incredible. Many of these kids will one day play in the MLB. I was able to travel a little and watch exceptional baseball.

In Fall during my chemo treatments, the former baseball coach and San Diego Hall of Famer, David Glassey, invited me to coach the seventh- and eighth-grade flag football B teams. I accepted. It was very enjoyable; the kids were fantastic. Parker is a wonderful school. I cannot say enough about them.

At the start of 2020, I saw that the Padres were hiring for the grounds crew. This had always been my dream job since I had been taking care of fields since I was fifteen. One of my players' dads had a contact, and I was called in for an interview by the head groundskeeper, Matt Balough. The interview went well. One hour after I had gotten home from the last cystoscopy, the Padres called and I was hired. It was a remarkable day. I started as soon as I had my background check.

Petco Park has a monster-truck rally every year, where the field is covered with dirt. After it ends, the dirt is taken out, and new grass is put down. The entire field is rebuilt. As a baseball guy, it was amazing to watch. It was very hard work and took a few days. At the end of it was the time COVID-19 was spreading and everything was shut down. It was a long wait to go back. I was in the age bracket for COVID-19 complications and had been battling cancer. I did not work. I had my two shots in January and started back in March. The crew is outstanding, and I am prejudiced, but I think they are the best in baseball. Matt Balough supervises everything and is the very best. Pete Hayes handles the infield. He will be a headman one day, and whichever team hires him will be lucky. Rob Cantwell handles the assignments and does a lot of the mound and plate work. When you are able to see what these guys do and how they do it, baseball fans would be greatly appreciative. I was truly lucky to work there.

In the first game I was able to work, I was sent out to pick up grass clippings right before the national anthem. They made the announcement "to please stand and remove your hat." I was on the field for the anthem. When it was over, I looked and Manny Machado was right behind me. It was at that moment that my entire lifetime dream had been reached. Although it was not as a player, I had finally made it to the show. I had a tear in my eye and wiped it out immediately, so no one could see. It does not sound like much, but for me it was massive.

I got to see great baseball and worked a couple of concerts. The work was not easy for me. I had done things for so long by myself, and I had to learn a new way of doing it. The Padres organization is outstanding, and there is no better place to work than Petco. For a guy who grew up in a little town in Oregon and always dreamed about playing in the MLB, this was as close as I could come. It was the best thing to be able to drive to an MLB park and work. I will never forget it. There are so many things about this job that are fantastic as a baseball fan. We would get to watch five to six innings, depending on how much work needed to be done. We got to go on the field after the third and sixth inning to drag and replace the bases and rake the field. One day during a game, Padres legend Randy Jones came down and talked to a few of our old guys. I only talked to players if they spoke first. Maybe because I was older, I was always treated excellently by the players and coaches, both home and away teams. I heard and saw a lot. When I was growing up I read that the code of baseball was "What you see here, what you say here, stays here." I have always believed in that, and I will not repeat what I heard.

On my way to work at the end of July for a game against the A's, I was broadsided at an intersection by a woman who ran a stop sign. I continued to work, but the pain was excruciating. I worked a game during the last home stand against the Giants. I could not move for two days after. I decided to let my body see if the time off would improve. Petco was due to put down new turf for the Holiday

73

Bowl, and I knew that I could not do the job. I had to resign from the best job I have ever had.

After everything settled, my divorce was final, and I moved back to Oregon. I did some substitute teaching. I also returned to the basketball court. I worked about fifty games and had a couple of ejections and many Ts. I guess being away for a while, I have a bunch of new coaches and players to be introduced to.

Life goes on, and I love each and every day. I look forward to tomorrow and the challenges that it provides.

ABOUT THE AUTHOR

Coming from a small town in Oregon, Mike Reed worked in three professional sports and coached high school and college baseball. This book is a collection of the many stories that have occurred over his career.

CPSIA information can be obtained
at www.ICGtesting.com
Printed in the USA
BVHW070839240323
661078BV00002B/302